Enneagram Self-Discovery

Easy-to-Follow Essential Guide on How to Uncover your Unique Path with the 9 Enneagram Personality Types to Build Self-Awareness and Achieve Personal Growth

Morgan Christopher Hudson

© **Copyright 2019 by Morgan Christopher Hudson - All rights reserved.**

The contents of this book may not be reproduced, duplicated or transmitted without direct written permission from the author.

Under no circumstances will any legal responsibility or blame be held against the publisher for any reparation, damages, or monetary loss due to the information herein, either directly or indirectly.

Legal Notice:

This book is copyright protected. This is only for personal use. You cannot amend, distribute, sell, use, quote or paraphrase any part or the content within this book without the consent of the author.

Disclaimer Notice:

Please note the information contained within this document is for educational and entertainment purposes only. Every attempt has been made to provide accurate, up to date and reliable complete information. No warranties of any kind are expressed or implied. Readers acknowledge that the author is not engaging in the rendering of legal, financial, medical or professional advice. The content of this book has been derived from various sources. Please consult a licensed professional before attempting any techniques outlined in this book.

By reading this document, the reader agrees that under no circumstances are is the author responsible for any losses, direct or indirect, which are incurred as a result of the use of information contained within this document, including, but not limited to, —errors, omissions, or inaccuracies.

Table of Contents

Introduction

Chapter 1: Getting Started with Enneagram Personality Types

Chapter 2: Discovering Your Enneagram Personality Type

Chapter 3: The 9 Personality Types Explained

Chapter 4: The Three Main Centers Explained

Chapter 5: Seeking Integrity and Balance – Type One

Chapter 6: Love is the Desire – Type Two

Chapter 7: Being Valued -Type Three

Chapter 8: Being Unique to Themselves – Type Four

Chapter 9: Achieving Understanding – Type Five

Chapter 10: Finding Reassurance – Type Six

Chapter 11: Seeking Contentment – Type Seven

Chapter 12: Protecting Oneself – Type Eight

Chapter 13: Having Peace of Mind – Type Nine

Chapter 14: Putting it All Together

Bonus Chapter: How to Apply Personality Types to Relationships

Conclusion

Introduction

In this book, you will learn how to discover yourself. You may think you already know yourself, but many people are living in ignorance of the anxiety, stress, negativity, fear, and anger that they are purposefully pushing away and ignoring. Yet, these emotions are still a part of them and affecting their daily lives, their emotional and spiritual health, and their relationships.

With the Enneagram personality method, you can learn about your individual personality type, wing types, the Triads, the three Centers, and how to put all of this information together for a better and healthier life. There is even a bonus chapter to help you apply this information to both your platonic and romantic relationships!

You don't have to settle for a life full of stress and disappointments, you can live your life to the fullest while enjoying the balance that comes from self-awareness.

Chapter 1: Getting Started with Enneagram Personality Types

Chapter 1: Getting Started with Enneagram Personality Types

You may have heard of the Enneagram personality types from a friend or a co-worker. Maybe you heard about it in another book, at religious practices, on television, or at work. Whatever piqued your interest on the Enneagram personality types, you can use them to benefit you through all aspects of life.

You can grow stronger as a person and become more balanced. But first, what is the Enneagram method? If you heard about it elsewhere, it may have seemed complex. But don't worry. You will learn all about Enneagram here in a straightforward and enjoyable process!

In psychology, the human mind, consciousness, and unconsciousness combine to form what is known as the human psyche. It is believed that the nine personality types in the Enneagram method are closely tied to the human psyche. Because of this, we all have one of these nine types as the main point in our personality from birth. This impacts our temperament and dominant personality traits.

This personality type that we have from birth is known as our dominant type. While it is possible to have multiple types, one will usually be dominant. This is especially true during childhood.

This dominant personality type will influence our emotions, thoughts, and behavior as a child. This process shapes our entire childhood and influences who we become as adults.

Although you may see yourself in several different types, maybe even all of them, you will have one main type. This is the type that influences you the most throughout your life. This type is the most important for you to understand to gain control and balance over your life.

Talking with other people of the same Enneagram type as yourself, you may be confused. After all, this person seems to be completely different from you! But this does not mean that you or they were mistakenly typed. In fact, while people of the same type will share certain characteristics, they can be quite different as well. Our mental health, fears and anxieties, and life experiences can cause us to be different, even if we are the same type as another person.

Our individualistic traits might also be impacted by some of the other types. For instance, if you are a type Five, then you could have many traits of type Four or type Six. This is because these two types are directly next to the Five and share some commonalities. These types are known as your wing types, and they help you to remain balanced.

The personality types in order of One to Nine are the Reformer, the Helper, the Achiever, the Individualist, the Investigator, the Loyalist, the Enthusiast, the Challenger, and the Peacemaker.

You may now understand the most basic aspects of the Enneagram method, but everything has a story. Just like everything else, this is true for the Enneagram personality types and their origins.

The Enneagram method and personality types have a long and rich history from a myriad of ancient traditions and wisdom. All of these beautiful insights from ancient cultures were combined by the Bolivian Oscar Ichazo. Along with being raised in his home country of Bolivia, Ichazo spent much time in Peru during his childhood. However, as an adult, he moved to Argentina. This is where he studied at a school of inner work. His studies at this school would shape him and inspire him to create the Enneagram method. In fact, soon after he completed his studies at this school, he traveled to Asia. While there, he continued his studies on culture, religion, and a person's very being. After Asia, Ichazo journeyed to South America. This is when he first began to write down the Enneagram methods and types by using everything he had learned from around the globe.

Then, in the late '60s and early '70s, Ichazo officially created the Arica School. The purpose of this school was to be a school of knowledge, which has traditionally been employed by the Greek, Buddhists, Sufi, and Hindu to provide enlightenment. It became a school with deep and interwoven teachings focusing on spirituality, cosmology, psychology, metaphysics, and more.

Well-known psychologists and writers have even visited the Arica School such as John Lilly and Claudio Naranjo. While there, they were able to learn Ichazo's methods of self-realization firsthand. Lilly and Naranjo were taught the fundamentals of the system and even engaged in their practices.

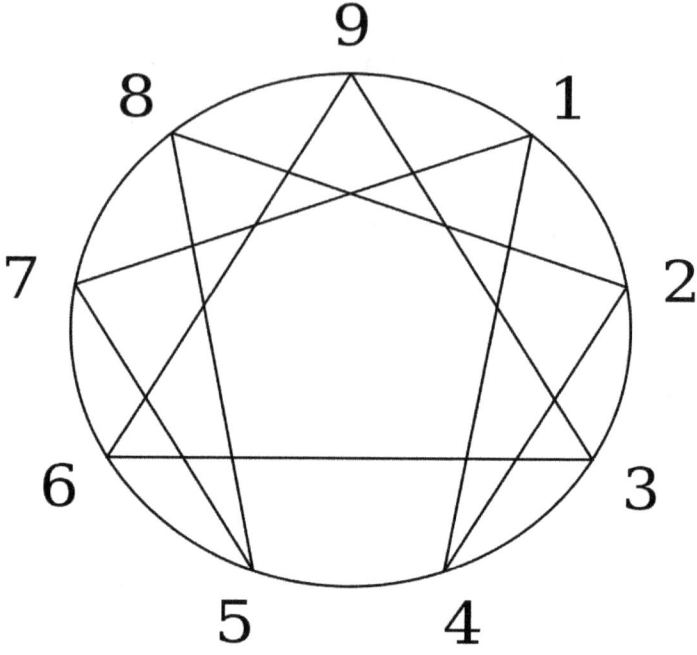

Many people incorrectly believe that George Gurdjieff was the one to develop the Enneagram method and the corresponding nine personality types.

This is because the ancient symbol of the Enneagram, as shown in the image, had been lost in modern society. However, the symbol that is the foundation of the Enneagram personality method was reintroduced into society by Gurdjieff at his own school of inner work, which was highly influential. He would teach the symbol of the Enneagram through a series of movements and dances. The purpose of this was to give his students a profound sense of meaning for the symbol and that which it represents.

Yet, it is clear that Gurdjieff did not teach his students the personality types and their method, as Ichazo did. The only teaching close to the personality types that Gurdjieff taught was the Chief Feature. He described this as being the characteristics that most define a person, their ego. But, unlike Ichazo, Gurdjieff used the Sufi method to communicate their Chief Feature. He would do this by telling the person what their most prominent faults were.

Due to this, many people early on mistakenly believed that it was George Gurdjieff who began the Enneagram personality method. This led to a widespread misunderstanding for decades on who the true originator actually was. While the method may have been inspired by a number of religions, it was Ichazo who combined all of the knowledge with the Enneagram method and first taught it.

There may be helpful personality typing systems that have a number of various types, most commonly three, four, or sixteen. But, the Enneagram method is different from these types at a foundational level.

Rather than being a simple list of various personalities, the Enneagram system is based on holistic symmetry and mathematics. This simple yet detailed design uses lines to represent the ways that energy can move in patterns.

When this ancient diagram is applied to people, it shows that we have many psychological patterns that can be revealed by the lines of the Enneagram.

By using this ancient symbol, Ichazo was able to further examine the human soul. More specifically, he found ways in which our soul and thinking becomes distorted, affecting our ego. When developing his theories about this, he greatly relied on Western philosophies. One of the most prominent of these philosophies was the idea of nine divine forms discussed by Plato in Platonic Solids or The Divine Forms.

Through Ichazo's development of this method, we have been able to learn that the Enneagram is an intertwining of lines that can move and influence us. By following these lines, we can further discover the interactions and influences that we can expect from other personality types within the system. While we are born with a main or dominant type which remains constant, we are able to be pushed or pulled along the lines of the Enneagram. Once we have moved along the lines, we can experience a significant change in our point of view or perspective. We may become able to respond to situations and the world around us in new ways we previously wouldn't have. This means that the lines can help us further explore our psyche. Through the lines, we can learn more about ourselves and find a new sense of balance and development.

It's understandable to be skeptical of the

Enneagram method. After all, it's a mystery to us how it is able to predict people's behavior. Most of us are uninterested in New Age beliefs with no scientific proof. But, just because the Enneagram method is once again gaining attention doesn't mean that it is New Age mumbo-jumbo. Don't believe me? What's the harm in testing out this method in your own life? You will soon see the results and benefits. You don't have to take my word for it, you can take it into your own hands. Hundreds of thousands of people long before you have received benefits from using the Enneagram method within their own lives, and it is now your turn.

We recently mentioned that there are a number of different personality typing systems. That raises the question, how does the Enneagram personality method compare to one of the most hyped personality tests, the Myers-Briggs (MBTI) method?

There are various foundational differences between the two types. One of these is the distinction of nature versus nurture and their effects on a person's personality. While these systems teach that both nature and nurture have an effect on a person, they teach them in different ways and their opinion on these aspects differ.

Neither Myers-Briggs or C. Jung who was influential in its creation discussed or wrote on the subject of nurture on more than a rare occasion. They taught that our personalities are largely nature, something that we are born with. Whereas they believed nurture was simply a compensation to help us manage in society. For instance, an introvert may learn to compensate in situations that are largely extroverted.

While the Enneagram method also teaches that we are born with our personality types by nature, they largely emphasize the effects that nurture has upon our psyche. Looking back on your childhood, you may be able to see how certain events and the way they impacted who you are today. This is how nurture affects us.

When discussing our psychological health, both

methods of personality typing have something to say.

With MBTI, it is believed that people have both prominent and inferior functions. This could mean that someone is more feeling than analytical or vice versa. But, some people may behave unknowingly repressing their "inferior" function, which is needed in order to be whole.

On the other hand, with the Enneagram method, you can learn your propensity for specific core vices, which impact your choices and reactions. This may mean that you are more prone to pride, envy, or another vice. But by learning what vice you are most prone to, you can learn to become more balanced.

Myers-Briggs may tell you how you think, take in information, and make decisions. But unlike the Enneagram method, it doesn't help you understand how you feel and why. MBTI may tell you what career you are most suited for, but it doesn't ask what motivates you the most or what causes your stress the most. Yet, with

Enneagram, you can learn the answers to these questions and more about yourself. You can learn things about yourself that you never recognized before.

Knowing ourselves is the key to changing and improving. We all have behaviors that become automatic. These can affect both ourselves and those around us. These behaviors may affect small day-to-day choices, or they could impact large life-changing choices. Either way, if we don't know ourselves, then we will remain stagnant and unbalanced.

The Enneagram personality method can show us the areas we are most likely to make mistakes, where we might get stuck, routine behaviors that we are oblivious to, and what's the biggest fear lying deep within our hearts might be.

Although, it doesn't only show the negative. The Enneagram can help push us forward, give us a deeper understanding to ourselves, increase our understanding and compassion towards others, help us to let go of damaging behaviors and patterns, and overall become the person that we want to be.

Rather than a static cookie cutter personality type, the Enneagram is a tool that shifts and flows as we do. By using this tool throughout our lives, we can reach our full potential, learn to use our inherent gifts, and fully engage in a life worth living. This process is often known as increasing our emotional intelligence, and it not only benefits ourselves but everyone around us.

The three main components of emotional intelligence are:

1. Having an emotional awareness of ourselves, where we can both identify and name our own emotions.

2. The ability to harness our emotions and apply them to various tasks such as solving a problem.

3. Managing emotions, both by being able to regulate our own and by having the ability to either calm down or cheer up

those around us.

As you can see, emotional intelligence is a simple concept, which we need to use on a daily basis. But just because the concept is simple doesn't mean it is actually simple to use. That is if we haven't been taught or aren't aware of how to harness or increase our emotional intelligence.

Some of the ways that having a higher emotional intelligence level may help you include:

- **You learn to better help others**
  One of the best ways we can impact the lives of others is by genuinely helping them. You may have many academic and professional accomplishments, but what will really impact a person is whether or not you are willing to help them. By learning to better help people, you can inspire them and build a more trusting relationship.
- **You can sincerely apologize**

When we are too prideful to admit to even small mistakes and especially the big ones, then the people around us take notice. They begin to trust us less and will feel pushed away. But when we gain a better understanding of ourselves, we are able to apologize with courage and strength. By showing humility, people will feel more comfortable and drawn toward you.

- **You can be authentic**

  Some people inaccurately believe that being authentic means that you share every part of yourself and your life to everyone. But this is a misconception brought about by lacking emotional intelligence. In truth, being authentic means that you truly believe what you say. That you stick to your principles and values. Not everyone appreciates authenticity. But in our technological age where it is difficult to tell truth from lie and friend from foe, being authentic is greatly valued.

- **Connect more**

    Having empathy means that we are able to understand others' feelings and thoughts. Rather than labeling or judging people, we can begin to see the world through their eyes. By doing this, we can not only better connect with those in our own lives, but people around the world.

    This doesn't mean you will always agree with a person, but you can deepen your understanding of them.

This is only a taste of what the Enneagram method can help you with. If you want to truly invest in your life and the lives of others, this book can help. But you can't simply read this book, you have to act on it. Purposefully learn your Enneagram personality type and practice self-awareness.

If you would like to learn more about the Enneagram method continue reading. You can also schedule time into your week to follow this chapter's Quick Start Action Step to learn more about the basics of the method.

Your Quick Start Action Step

This book has everything you need to understand the basics of the Enneagram method, learn more about your personality type, become increasingly balanced, and more. But that doesn't mean that there aren't other helpful resources out there as well. Check out these links in order to deepen your understanding of the Enneagram method!

- https://www.enneagraminstitute.com
- https://www.reddit.com/r/Enneagram/
- https://www.youtube.com/watch?v=xYuHYgoJels
- https://thoughtcatalog.com/heidi-priebe/2015/11/if-youre-confused-about-your-enneagram-type-read-this/

Chapter 2: Discovering Your Enneagram Personality Type

Chapter 2: Discovering Your Enneagram Personality Type

If you don't know where to begin when looking for an Enneagram test or how to interpret the results, don't worry. In this chapter, you will learn all you need to know to have confidence when choosing a test and reading the results.

Firstly, it is important to know that there are a lot of tests out there that were created by anyone off the street, just like those Facebook quizzes that tell you what type of pizza you are. These tests are inaccurate and will be unable to help you find your true Enneagram personality type. But don't worry! At the end of this chapter, in the Quick Start Action Step, I will provide you with an accurate test you can use.

There are many tests out there that will ask if you disagree, strongly disagree, somewhat agree, strongly agree, or are neutral. Each of the responses adds a point to a specific personality type or two, which is then added to your total. These tests are the most common because they are the easiest to create with the software available. These tests are usually not created by anyone accredited or even by someone anonymous. You are unlikely to get an accurate result out of these tests. If yours does happen to be accurate, it is most likely because these tests can't always be wrong. Statistically, they must be right on a rare occasion. But even if they are right, you won't know if you haven't taken an accurate test.

Some people will simply try to read through a list of traits that are common with the nine types to discover their individual personality type. The reason this is unreliable is that these descriptions can vary greatly depending on how the writer interpreted the characteristics. Not only that, but the traits and characteristics of the types may not fit a person one-hundred percent. This can lead a person to believe that they aren't their true personality type.

The method used by the most accurate test will force you to choose between one of two statements. Even if you don't feel strongly either way, you will have to figure out which option you slightly more toward. Think about it as if the eye doctor is asking you if options one or two are better. You may not be sure what the difference between the two lenses is, but you have to choose one of them.

At the end of the test, your score is added up and you can see a list of all of the types in order of how you scored on them. Most likely your highest score is your dominant type. But for people who are closely tied to two or three types, their dominant type may actually be one of the other types that they scored highly on.

You will score the highest on one of the following types:

- Type One: The Reformer
- Type Two: The Helper

- Type Three: The Achiever
- Type Four: The Individualist
- Type Five: The Investigator
- Type Six: The Loyalist
- Type Seven: The Enthusiast
- Type Eight: The Challenger
- Type Nine: The Peacemaker

When taking the official Enneagram test, it is usually rather obvious what your dominant personality type is. This is because your dominant type will most likely score three or four points higher than any of the other personality types. You can then confirm the type by reading over the personality's characteristics and traits, determining if they fit.

If you find that the characteristics don't fit you, then there are several factors that may have affected your score.

- When you have high scores across Five,

Four, and Three, it could mean that you are a type Six.

- Women who have a Two as the highest result may actually be one of their other high scoring types. This is because women are often taught by society to act as if they are type Two, even if it is not their dominant type.

- If you are unsure about your results, study the three highest scoring personality types, as one of them is most likely your dominant type.

- The culture, environment, and family that you grew up in during childhood may falsely affect your results. You may want to consider if your highest scoring personality type reflects the environment you grew up in. This type may be a part of who you are, but not necessarily your dominant type.

- If you find that your score is closely distributed between all nine types, there are two main causes that could affect this. The first is that you may lack a true understanding of yourself. The second is that you may have a very healthy sense of yourself. Maybe you have experienced the help therapeutically, spiritually, or even on your own with a deeper understanding of yourself.

- If you take the Enneagram test on multiple occasions, your dominant type should stay the same. Although, you may find that other types that you score highly on alter from time to time. This is because if you are struggling with something in life, your other types may vary. For instance, if you are struggling with your career, then you might find that your One, Three, and Eight personalities score higher than previously. If you are struggling with relationships within your life, then you might score either lower or higher in the Two, Six, or Nine personality type. This is because these three types are closely related to relationships. If you are struggling with a significant other or friend in your life, then it might affect your score. You will find that your test might slightly change once again once your career or relationship troubles resolve. Although, again, your dominant type should remain the same.

Your Quick Start Action Step

Learning about the Enneagram method is the first step along your journey, but the second step should be to learn your personality type because you are unable to receive the many benefits it has to offer without knowing your type. Check out one of these two websites to take a comprehensive test that will give you the knowledge you need to grow!

- www.integrative9.com/enneagram/
- https://tests.enneagraminstitute.com

Chapter 3: The 9 Personality Types Explained

Chapter 3: The 9 Personality Types Explained

We are now beginning to get to the truly transformative portion of this book. You will now learn about the actual nine personality types that we have discussed, wing types, and of course, a Quick Start Action Step to get you on your way to growth and balance.

The main nine personality types are the Reformer, the Helper, the Achiever, the Individualist, the Investigator, the Loyalist, the Enthusiast, the Challenger, and the Peacemaker. But before we go into an overview of all nine types, their strengths and weaknesses, their fears, and their real-life examples, let's explore wing types. This is important to go over because your wing type can slightly alter your Enneagram personality type.

The reason for this is because every person is

unique, we don't fit within a box. We can be a mixture of our dominant personality type, along with having traits from the personality type next to us. This means that if you are a Five, you could have traits of a Four or a Six. If you are a One, you might have traits of a Nine or a Two. The types that are next to our number are known as wings.

While your primary personality type will display the dominant traits, you may also have side traits from your wing type that add to your individuality. These side traits may complement your personality or appear contradictory. This is because people, and our personalities, are multi-faceted. We are not static or two-dimensional.

This means that you don't only need to consider your dominant type, but your wing type as well. Your personality as a whole, including your strengths, weaknesses, and fears will be best understood when you consider all of the applying factors. If you are a Six and find there are some areas of your personality that aren't explained, it may mean that those parts of you are due to your wing type of Seven or Eight.

While some people show only one wing, others may show only a few signs of having a wing type at all. Even rarer are people who are greatly influenced by not one, but both wing types.

Studies on people who have two prevalent wings have shown that this, while fully possible, is rare. In a sense, everyone has two wings, as there are always two personality numbers on your sides. But it is rare for someone to display traits of both of these wings. Instead, it is more common for one wing to lie dormant while the other one affects a person's personality.

This means that if you are a Three, you may have both One and Two next to your type, but only adopt aspects of one of these types. Whichever wing that your personality takes on can greatly alter how you function, your fears, and strengths. Eights with Seven wings are greatly different than Eights with Nine wings.

Many people, after studying the Enneagram, training, and growth have found that they developed a second wing. Meaning, that if they are a Six, they are displaying traits of both a Five and a Seven as well. This may be because after undergoing self-evaluation, psychological work, and spiritual growth, a person begins to mature and develops the ability to travel between the nine personality types including their other wing. Or it could be that as the person ages and grows that they specifically developed their second wing. Either way, this is a sign of growth and progress toward becoming more balanced and emotionally healthy.

Now that you understand what the wings are, let's explore the basics of the nine personality types of the Enneagram.

Type One: The Reformer

One is characterized by having a strong instinct for right and wrong. They are ethical, conscientious, advocates, and crusaders. Yet while they desire to make a change for the better, they are afraid that they might make a mistake along the way. Their high standards can lead to resentment, impatience, and perfectionism. But when emotionally healthy and balanced, a One is well-organized, noble, wise, kind, and discerning.

Main Fear: That they will be condemned, make mistakes, or be overcome with 'evil.'

One with a Nine-Wing Enneagram: The Idealist

One with a Two-Wing Enneagram: The Advocate

Real Life Examples of Ones: Celine Dion, Katherine Hepburn, Plato, Michelle Obama, Kate Middleton, Tina Fey, Meryl Streep, Jeanne d'Arc, Harrison Ford, Al Gore, Jimmy Carter, Martha Stewart, Hilary Clinton, Anita Roddick, Julie Andrews, Jane Fonda, Maggie Smith, Helen Hunt, Margaret Thatcher, Nelson Mandela, Prince Charles, Emma Thompson.

Type Two: The Helper

The second personality type is known to be warmhearted, kind, empathetic, friendly, generous, sincere, sentimental, and self-sacrificing. However, they can sometimes be overly people pleasing, possibly giving false flattery and trying to gain acceptance. They can struggle to acknowledge their own needs and use the attention they gain from others to validate themselves. But when balanced, a Two can offer unconditional love and support. They are known to be incredibly selfless and giving.

Main Fear: They fear deep within their heart that they are unworthy of love and unwanted.

Two with a One-Wing Enneagram: The Servant

Two with a Three-Wing Enneagram: The Hostess/Host

Real Life Examples of Twos: John Denver, Pope John XXIII, Eleanor Roosevelt, Stevie Wonder, Dolly Parton, Mary Kay Ash, Monica Lewinsky, Nancy Reagan, Martin Sheen, Arsenio Hall, Lionel Richie, Josh Groban, Ann

Landers, Elizabeth Taylor.

Type Three: The Achiever

Threes are charming and self-assured, attracting a large crowd and are known as the life of a party. They are known to be energetic, conscious of status, competent, poised, driven, and diplomatic. Although an unhealthy Three is overly concerned with their image and what everyone thinks of them. They have a strong need to distinguish themselves and receive affirmation. This means that they can easily be overly competitive and obsess over work to an unhealthy degree. But when they are emotionally healthy, they can learn to accept themselves, become authentic, and are strong role models.

Main Fear: That they are 'nobody' with no personality, need, or significance. They often feel worthless and unneeded.

Three with a Two-Wing Enneagram: The Charmer

Three with a Four-Wing Enneagram: The Professional

Real Life Examples of Threes: Lance Armstrong, Lady Gaga, Elvis Presley, Bill Clinton, Prince William, Madonna, Whitney Houston, Tom Cruise, John Edwards, Muhammad Ali, Augustus Caesar, Anne Hathaway, Reese Witherspoon, Justin Bieber, Will Smith, Taylor Swift, Tiger Woods, Oprah Winfrey, Tony Robbins, Paul McCartney, Ryan Secrest.

Type Four: The Individualist

The Fourth personality type is known to be personable, honest, sensitive, reserved, self-aware, and creative. But they can also struggle with feelings of self-pity, moodiness, self-consciousness, melancholy, and self-indulgence. They may keep others at a distance to avoid feelings of vulnerability. A Four may even avoid society and feel distrust and disdain for it. Yet, when balanced, a Four is inspirational, creative, stable, brave, and strong. Fours enjoy being able to surround themselves with beauty, be freely creative, and focus on their individuality.

Main Fear: That they are 'nobody' with no personality, need, or significance.

Four with a Three-Wing Enneagram: The Aristocrat

Four with a Five-Wing Enneagram: The Bohemian

Real Life Examples of Fours: Hank Williams, Cher, Nicolas Cage, Tchaikovsky, Kat Von D., Angelina Jolie, Anne Frank, Billie Holiday, Bob Dylan, Prince, Amy Winehouse, Johnny Depp, Sarah McLachlan, Cat Stevens, Virginia Woolf, Jackie Kennedy, Tennesse Williams, Edgar Allen Poe, Leonard Cohen, Kate Winslet.

Type Five: The Investigator

Fives are known to excel when it comes to focus, concentration, and both processing and developing complex skills and ideas. They can be insightful, curious, innovative, independent, alert, and inventive. Although, these strengths can also lead to Fives becoming detached, intense, isolated, eccentric, high-strung, cynical of spirituality, and preoccupied with their mind rather than living in society. But, if a Five can learn to overcome their weaknesses, they can be pioneers of thought, imagination, science, and more. They have a unique ability to see the world in a new way, which often puts them ahead of their time.

Main Fear: Being incompetent, incapable, useless, and helpless.

Five with a Four-Wing Enneagram: The Iconoclast

Five with a Six-Wing Enneagram: The Problem Solver

Real Life Examples of Fives: Emily Dickinson, Mark Zuckerberg, Gautama Buddha, Bill Gates, Albert Einstein, Stephen King, Alfred Hitchcock, Tim Burton, John Nash, Agatha Christie, Vincent van Gogh, Glenn Gould, David York, Stephen Hawking.

Type Six: The Loyalist

The sixth type is known for being committed, reliable, cooperative, responsible, trustworthy, and hard-working. They are wonderful at foreseeing potential problems and then troubleshooting in order to solve it before it occurs. Their downfall is that they can become highly stressed, anxious, defensive and evasive. All the while, they often complain about it to those around them. A Six can struggle with suspicious, self-doubt, indecisiveness, rebelliousness, and are defiant. But, when a Six is emotionally healthy, they can be incredibly self-reliant, stable, and encourage all those around them.

Main Fear: Losing guidance or support

Six with a Five-Wing Enneagram: The Defender

Six with a Seven-Wing Enneagram: The Buddy

Real Life Examples of Sixes: Julia Roberts, Ellen Page, Robert De Niro, Prince Harry,

Malcolm X, Mark Twain, Princess Diana, Eminem, Marilyn Monroe, Tom Hanks, Chris Rock, Sigmund Freud, Meg Ryan, Jay Leno, Mel Gibson, Jennifer Aniston, Hugh Laurie.

Type Seven: The Enthusiast

Sevens are known to be full of optimism and spontaneity. They can be extroverted, spirited, and playful. Yet, they are also versatile and practical. These traits, when unbalanced, can lead Sevens to become distracted, scattered, over-extended, and undisciplined. They are constantly seeking out new acclivities and distractions, which leaves them exhausted and anxious. They are unable to sit still, leaving them impulsive and impatient. But, when a Seven is emotionally healthy and balanced, they are great achievers and talented. They can truly enjoy life and feel satisfied.

Main Fear: That they may be deprived or experience pain.

Seven with a Six-Wing Enneagram: The Entertainer

Seven with an Eight-Wing Enneagram:
The Realist

Real Life Examples of Sevens: Amelia Earhart, Elton John, Katy Perry, Fred Astaire, Bruce Willis, Howard Stern, Robert Downey Jr., Thomas Jefferson, George Clooney, Simon Cowell, Leonardo DiCaprio, Brad Pitt, Joe Biden, Galileo Galilei, Cary Grant, Chuck Berry, Mozart.

Type Eight: The Challenger

Eights are known for being resourceful, decisive, assertive, self-confident, and straight-forward. Although, they can also be domineering and selfish. An Eight will feel that they must control their entire environment, including their work, personal life, and relationships. This can lead to them becoming intimidating, confrontational, and loose tempers. They do this in order to protect their own heart and emotions, but in the process, end up pushing everyone away. But a balanced and emotionally healthy type Eight can learn to be inspiring, generous, self-controlled, and brave.

Main Fear: Being controlled or harmed.

Eight with a Seven-Wing Enneagram: The Maverick

Eight with a Nine-Wing Enneagram: The Bear

Real Life Examples of Eights: Franklin D. Roosevelt, Paul Newman, Alex Baldwin, Rosie O'Donnell, Winston Churchill, Donald Trump, John Wayne, Dr. Phil, Martin Luther King Jr., Serena Williams, Queen Latifah, Russell Crowe.

Type Nine: The Peacemaker

Nines are often characterized by their warm and friendly personality. They are supportive, optimistic, trusting, accepting, creative, and stable individuals. However, they can become easily complacent with situations, as they are overly willing to keep the peace. Even if that false sense of peace is detrimental. A Nine's deepest desire is to be free of conflict. They desire everything to go smoothly and will tend to minimize the effect of anything problematic that they wish to ignore. A Nine is often willing to stubbornly allow their life to become stagnant rather than choosing an uncomfortable or confrontational approach to fix things.

When a Nine is emotionally healthy and balanced, they can be wonderful true peacemakers. Even if a situation is difficult, they can be willing to face it in order to address the issues. They shine at bringing people together, embracing differences, and standing their ground.

Main Fear: Separation and Loss

Nine with a One-Wing Enneagram: The Dreamer

Nine with an Eight-Wing Enneagram: The Referee

Real Life Examples of Nines: Zooey Deschanel, Queen Elizabeth II, Walt Disney, Abraham Lincoln, Claude Monet, Ronald

Reagan, George W. Bush, Gloria Steinem, James Taylor, Jimmy Stewart, Toby McGuire, Morgan Freeman, Audrey Hepburn, Janet Jackson, George Lucus, Carl Jung, Whoopie Goldberg.

Your Quick Start Action Step

Now that you understand what wing types are and the basics of the Nine Enneagram personality types, you can better understand what your individual type is and how it affects you. You should already know what number your type is. Now, it is time to find and understand your wing types. Schedule time this week to study up on your wing types on both sides of your personality, and see how one, or both of them, might be influencing you.

Chapter 4:
The Three Main Centers Explained

Chapter 4: The Three Main Centers Explained

The nine Enneagram personalities are divided into three groups, each containing three of the personality types. These groups are known as Centers. There is the Instinctive Center which contains Eight, Nine, and One, the Feeling Center with Two, Three and Four and lastly, the Thinking Center with Five, Six, and Seven. Knowing which Center you belong in is as

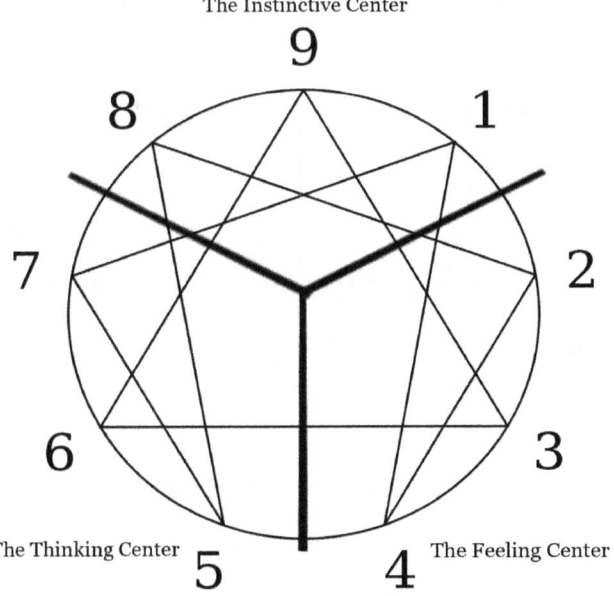

simple as knowing which personality type you are.

Each of these Centers and their personality types share specific traits. These traits may not always be obvious, but they are there. This is because each of the Centers and their personalities, known as Triads, has a collection of characteristics. These characteristics largely are subconscious, but can greatly affect a person. For instance, anger is common in the Instinctive Center. Shame is mostly felt by the Feeling Center. Lastly, Fear controls the Thinking Center. All nine personality types may experience these feelings and emotions. But a given emotion will most affect a person who's in a Center connected with it.

In order to see how this is all connected, you need to learn about the head, the heart, and the belly.

Riso and Hudson, those who developed the well-respected and most accurate form of the Enneagram test, have theorized about the

Three Centers and Triads. Their theory is that each of the nine Enneagram personality types is a direct result of a specific imbalance within the three Centers.

We aren't born with this imbalance. Instead, we are born in a state of balance and emotional well-being. While in this state, we are in-tune with our true nature and able to access the Essence within all three Centers.

When we are in this natural state and our Centers are balanced, then we are able to access all of the Essential qualities and live at a high level with ease. But then, we naturally develop an ego in order to survive within a difficult, harmful, and painful world. This development of the ego causes us to lose contact with part of our being, which causes much pain and damage to our psyche. Therefore, the ego attempts to compensate by developing its own way of staying into contact with the Essence.

The Centers are named for the Essence which the ego is responding with pain toward losing contact with. They can respond to this loss by manipulating energy within the Center in three different ways. This includes under-expressing energy, overexpressing, or both under and overexpressing in the case of personalities that have been the most disconnected.

The Belly/Instinctive Center

The Belly is all important, as it allows us to function in society. This Center of Intelligence is vital in order to interact with people, move and flow in life, and attain our goals. This Center controls our instincts and is what enables us to be truly connected to our bodies.

Many cultures have explored the connection between our instincts, feelings, and our belly. In Qigong, it's believed to be our source of willpower, vitality, and confidence. In Buddhism, it is respected as our source of intuition, intention, and will. Even Western researchers are now calling the belly the "second brain." They have partly named it thus because its nervous system is nearly of the same complexity as the human brain. But they have also found that it is greatly responsible for emotional regulation with the production of endorphins and serotonin.

This modern science confirms what spiritual teachers across the world, and the Enneagram, have been teaching all along. That is that our emotions don't originate within the heart, but instead within the belly. By the time these feelings and emotions reach our hearts, they are merely projections of what we have already felt. We are only thinking about our feelings rather than actually letting ourselves fully feel them within our belly.

But if we are able to tap into this Essence and live fully present and grounded without our Belly, then we can feel our emotions while they are at their most pure state.

People often believe that we connect to others, experience deep emotions, and love through our hearts. People might say "I'm putting my heart ahead of my mind, I'm in love." But it's not through our heart that we make these connections, rather the belly.

The truth is that connections dictated by the heart are superficial. You might experience a relationship with a seemingly deep connection, you are perfectly in sync, and completely understand the other person. Then suddenly one day, you realize that you never truly knew them, it was a small crush and nothing more. When this happens, it's because you were feeling with only your heart. To experience a truly deep and grounded relationship, we need to feel primarily with our belly.

When our ego has made us lose connection with our belly Center, we become unbalanced and lose our sense of grounding. We begin to feel that we no longer belong and that everyone and everything is infringing upon us. This process naturally leads us to feel that we want to affect the environment around us, rather than allowing it to affect us.

In order to compensate for a lack of grounding or ego will then step in and cause us to attempt to hide out problems and overcome them. This leads to aggression, resistance, control issues, repression, and bodily tension.

On the other hand, when our Belly center is healthy, we are able to experience the Essential qualities being effortlessly expressed. This includes a sense of strength and wholeness, a feeling of being grounded, confidence, connection, vulnerability, and engagement.

The types that are within the Belly Triad are the Eight, Nine, and One, which sit upon the top of the Enneagram symbol. This is why these types are most affected by anger, rage, and a need for autonomy.

The Heart/Feeling Center

The heart is important for falling in love with and recognizing the true nature of people and all else that is around us. In fact, it has been referred to as "the organ of knowing." People may think that knowledge all happens in the head, but the intelligence of the heart is important. This all-important organ helps us in realizing the truth, knowing who we truly are, sharing authentically, and share authentic soulful connections. Most of our feelings may originate in the belly, but it is our heart that allows us both to share and recognize the truth. Most people devalue love to some obligatory cheesy Valentine's Day Hallmark card. But true love is compassionate, powerful, cleansing, healing, freeing, and terrifying.

The reason that love has been devalued to such an extent is precisely that we have lost connection with our hearts. We are terrified of letting people see our true selves. We cynically believe that we are unworthy of love or even unlovable. A true love that is honest and authentic seems like such a fantasy that we water down the mere idea with a cheesy joke of its true nature.

By following this process, we are letting ourselves miss out on a powerful and healing part of life, and doing this by keeping our ego firmly rooted in place. By using our heart, we may be stripped of all our facades, bare and plain to see, but by doing this, we can remove our limitations. There is no need for false ideas of who we are and harmful thoughts of our worth. Instead, we need to allow ourselves to see the truth and reality, and in the process, we will free our souls and psyches.

Due to this disconnection with the heart, people begin to expect someone else to come along and save them. They see nothing worthy about themselves, so they rely on the other person to see it for them. The problem is, that won't truly help in a lasting way unless they reconnect with their heart and allow themselves to see the truth. That they have worth. Rather than rejecting yourself, you need to look at your soul and who you really are with open arms.

This disconnection with the heart occurs due to ego-splitting. Due to having a lack of experience of being valued that we are willing to trust in, we begin to believe that we are in fact of no value. Since we believe we have no worth, we create a fantasy version of ourselves that we see as somehow better and deserving. We will project this fantasy when we are feeling valuable, but it never helps since the fantasy never touches the heart. Deep down we know that this fantasy isn't our true self.

In our void of worthlessness, the ego will replace healthy feelings of honesty and genuineness with narcissism, overly emotional reactions, and the expectation that we will only feel valued if someone outside of ourselves can validate us.

When we are in the Heart Center, we become blind to our true nature, that of others, and our value.

When our heart is able to awaken and become both healthy and balanced, we will find that our Essential qualities freely flow. This includes authenticity, love, truth, beauty, gratitude, poignancy, delicacy, and impressionability. We can begin to truly understand unconditional love. Others are able to bathe in the love and connection that is flowing through us and into the world. We can begin to understand how we are connected to everything else.

The Enneagram types which are within the Triad of the heart are Two, Three, and Four. It is for this reason that these types share a commonality of searching for their inner value, shame, and a lack of trust in themselves.

The Head/Thinking Center

The head Center manages our perception, awareness, contemplation, intuition, insight, and inner guidance. By using our head center, we can intuitively understand the workings not only of society but the world and universe at large. It is the head that allows us to openly be aware of all that is around us and affecting us at a deeper level. It allows us to freely make decisions without being clouded by biases or distractions.

In order to benefit from this, we must learn to quiet our minds. This will allow us to pick up on subtle cues, signals, and impressions with clarity.

We may have a misconception that we think a lot. But, in reality, we are only allowing repetitive memories, opinions, and judgments circle around our minds endlessly for entertainment. In fact, ninety-eight percent of our so-called "thinking" is only repetitive ideas that have no value. Our minds hold an incredible amount of power to process information, yet instead, we use it to filter out information so that we only ever have to hear something that we already agree with. We play mental puzzles and go over theories and concepts, yet these have no value in the real world and won't help us in life.

You are not a rodent that needs to run endlessly on a wheel of repetitive ideas.

Through the ego-splitting of our Essence, we lose connection with the head Center. We begin to feel the loss of being grounded and notice that we are struggling with inner guidance. To remedy that, the ego steps in. To simply fill the void, but not fix the true problem, we begin to fill our minds with beliefs, opinions, strategy, cynicism, mental chatter, mistrust, and anxiety about decision making.

We begin to feel threatened and that we need to quickly find something new to place our trust in. It feels as if life is a vicious predator on the prowl and waiting to attack. We begin to focus on the outer world, in search of the threat. This leads to us experiencing the world through our thoughts about it, rather than truly experiencing it in a pure and direct form.

When our head Center is balanced and healthy, we can experience a true type of stillness. This will leave us receptive, free from anxiety, and delighted with the way we can directly experience our impressions. We can get in touch with a new type of clarity, innate brilliance that had previously been dormant, and astounding wisdom.

We will begin to experience the Essence of our head with ease. This includes peace, support, wonder, stillness, wisdom, clarity, and more. The head center and our mind are directly responsible for the perception of the world around us and our inner selves, guidance, and trust.

The personality triad within the Head Center is the Five, Six, and Seven personality types. It is for this reason that these types often struggle with uncertainty, dread, and anxiety. They lack the inner guidance and the grounded experience that the head offers.

The Directional Arrows

Look again at the Enneagram symbol placed at the beginning of this chapter. Notice anything about it? All of the lines lead somewhere. A line leads from one personality type to the next. This is not a coincidence. Like everything else about the shape of the Enneagram, there is profound meaning behind it.

As you already know, none of the personality types are static. We change based on our environments, thoughts, feelings, insecurities or confidences, society, and the lies or truths that we tell ourselves. The direction of the lines on the Enneagram denote where our personality is at, both in terms of stagnation and growth. This is why each personality is connected to two lines, which then connects to two other personalities.

The first line attached to our personality number is the Direction of Growth. By following this line, we can see how a person is likely to act as they become more mature, self-aware, and balanced.

The second line is the Direction of Stress. By following this line, you can see how a certain personality type will react when they are under pressure or increased stress.

This once again displays the beauty and flexibility of the Enneagram. It doesn't believe in putting people in boxes. Rather, it is a symbol of how people feel, think, and react.

The Direction of Stress is easy to remember because you can simply look at the Enneagram and follow the lines to find which number goes from one to the next. But these lines could go in two directions, so how do you know which direction to start? The order is simple. One, Four, Two, Eight, Five, Seven, One. This shows that most Ones will act like a Four under stress, a Four like a Two, a Two like an Eight, an Eight like a Five, a Five like a Seven, a Seven like a One, and the cycle repeats itself.

There is a triangle in the middle of the Enneagram, this line sequence for the Direction of Stress is Nine to Six, Six to Three, Three to Nine. The Direction of Growth is the same sequence but in reverse. This means that a stable and emotionally One will act like a Seven, a Seven a Five, a Five an Eight, an Eight a Two, a Two a Four, and a Four a One.

The sequence for the Direction Growth on the triangular lines is Nine to Three, Three to Six, Six to Nine.

Whether you are a Three, a Five, a Six, or another personality type, your Direction of

Stress and Direction of Growth will both impact you greatly. If you hope to gain a complete idea of your personality, wing, and Center, you also need to include your directional arrows. All of these things together are what build your personality as a whole. You cannot see the complete painting without taking in all of its pieces.

For instance, someone isn't simply a type Five. They are a Five with a Four-wing or a Six-wing. They are in the head/thinking Center. Their Direction of Stress leads to Seven and their Direction of Growth leads to Eight. All of these elements as a whole are an important part of who they are.

As we become more balanced, mature, and emotionally healthy, we will ideally learn to move around the entire symbol of the Enneagram. This will enable us to integrate the benefits of each of the personality types within our own. The Enneagram isn't about where we are in there here and now, but rather where we are trying to get to.

The way you need to focus on developing and growing does not only vary depending on what Center you are in but on your specific personality type. This is because each type struggles with different fears, anxieties, avoidance issues, distrusts, self-confidence or lack thereof, and more. You can see detailed ideas on how to grow in the chapter on your personality type. But in the meantime, try the following Quick Start Action Step to becoming increasingly grounded and balanced.

Your Quick Start Action Step

Schedule a time this week where you will have no interruptions and focus on your well-being and growth. It may take some time out of your personal life, but it will be more than worth the time you put into it. Do you want to live a stagnant live ungrounded and full of anxiety? Or would you rather flourish and allow all of your strengths to shine brightly?

- Write out a list of your personality's known weaknesses.

- Clear your mind and practice a few minutes of deep breathing exercises.

- Now that your mind is clear from all of the distractions, meditate on the list. Don't just think "Is this true? Of course, it isn't." Instead, look at the list with an open mind and spend a minimum of five minutes examining each listed weakness.

- If you feel even the slightest twinge that you might have that weakness, then you should highlight it to focus on further.

- Once you have your list, you will know which areas to first begin working on improving. You may not have been able to see all of them, many of us don't see ourselves honestly, but that's okay.

- As you work on improving the areas you can see need improvement, you will grow more balanced and be able to more easily notice and recognize your other flaws without blame or anxiety.

Chapter 5: Seeking Integrity and Balance – Type One

Chapter 5: Seeking Integrity and Balance – Type One

The first of the personality types was dubbed The Reformer because they have a strong sense of justice. They often feel as if their life is a mission, and want to improve upon the world in a number of ways. Even if they have little influence outside of their social sphere, they will improve upon what they can. They may face adversity, but they strive to overcome it. They will take on moral adversity in order to improve the world and make a meaningful difference. While it may cost them much physically, emotionally, and financially, they often strive to attain a higher value for the world.

Due to the strong sense of purpose that Ones often feel, they will often have the need to justify their opinions and actions not only to themselves but to those around them as well. This means that they will spend much time reflecting on themselves and the results of their actions.

Ones often believe that they are someone who lives solely off of objective truth and logic, though this is not necessarily true. Rather, they are people who are passionate and have a strong instinct of what they believe is right. They use these convictions to judge and rationalize themselves and their following actions.

Ones deeply desire to be useful to those around them and the world in general. Even if the thought is only barely conscious, they should feel that they have a mission that they must accomplish. This mission can be some grand-scale task such as reforming the country, something more moderate in size such as saving the lives of animals in local shelters or by going vegan, or something small such as reducing the chaos and disorder in their environment.

Ones often repress their desires and instinctual drives in order to stay true to their mission and principles. They are reluctant to share these thoughts and desires with others. Because of this, Ones often are seen as people who are incredibly self-controlled and even rigid. Due to their struggles with repression, they can also have difficulties with resistance and aggression.

While others may see Ones as rigid and self-controlled, they feel otherwise about themselves. In fact, they feel as if they are boiling over with their desires and passions. If they don't hold back, they feel that they, and everyone around them, will regret it.

Ones strive for a sense of being "perfect" that is impossible to attain. But they believe if they are able to reach this state of "perfection" that they will not only be justified in the eyes of others but in their own eyes as well.

Sadly, by trying to reach this state of perfection, they often punish themselves and create a personal hell. They overly criticize much of what they do, think, and who they are. Ones see their mistakes everywhere like fallen leaves. Because of this, Ones often struggle to trust themselves and their sense of right from wrong. This leads them to trust in their superego, which is what they learned during childhood.

When Ones become unbalanced and too ingrained in their singular personality, they often seem severe and unforgiving. Learning to depart from this while still following their sense of justice is important for the growth of a One.

There are many Ones throughout history who sacrificed much in order to accomplish a grand goal. While a One doesn't have to achieve something enormous, there are many throughout history who left their mark. Jeanne d'Arc left her French village in order to help restore the country to its people and out of the hands of the British.

A Swedish architect, Raoul Wallenberg, left his safe and comfortable life to save Jews during World War II. During the Siege of Budapest, Wallenberg was captured by the Soviet Red Army and disappeared. After being imprisoned for a couple of years, he died, and much of what happened to him during that time was a mystery. Despite the suffering Wallenberg went through, he was able to save the lives of tens of thousands of Jews in Nazi-occupied Hungary.

Gandhi was a successful lawyer, but he left behind his career and family in order to help his country. Despite being imprisoned on many occasions due to his activism, Gandhi continued to fight for the independence of India from the British. Once India did gain its independence, largely due to his efforts, there are many people of Hindu, Sikh, and Muslim religion who were displaced from their homes. This caused much violence. In order to calm the country, Gandhi visited the areas most affected by violence in order to provide spiritual healing. He even took on hunger strikes to impact those who were fighting. One of these fast he completed when he was seventy-eight.

While a type One can certainly live out a peaceful and happy life, during times of great need, many of them feel that it is their mission to follow their sense of justice.

Ones in Relation to Their Center

In the previous chapter, we mentioned that within a Center each Triad will experience either under-expressing energy, overexpressing energy, or both under and overexpressing energy. For the One this means that they under express energy in order to try to remain stable after the ego-splitting.

Ones believe that they aren't good enough because they lost their grounding and trust that lies within the primal nature of belly energy. Yet, their psyche isn't accepting more belly energy. It is seen as a threat, so the One denies its own nature and existence. This leaves a One repressing their natural needs and the expression of their belly energy.

The way the belly energy is blocked is much the same as a clogged pipe. Something is cutting it off from reaching its destination, but the pressure continues to build and build. That is until it inevitably finds a way to release. For an unhealthy One, this is likely to be expressed in destructive ways. After all, a clogged pipe doesn't just fix itself. It will burst in order to get the release it needs. A One will either justify the unhealthy ways in which they cope, or ignore them completely.

Thankfully, a healthy One is comfortable with their Belly energy. This means that they are able to find constructive ways in which to express themselves.

Personal Growth

- It is important to learn to take it easy and relax. Allow yourself to escape and take some time for yourself. During this time, don't allow yourself to think that everything is up to you and that if you take time off, it will be a disaster. The world is not up to one person alone, you can rely on other people.

- It is easy to let yourself get emotionally invested and angry about the wrongdoings of others. Sometimes they may genuinely be wrong, but what is the point of you damaging your own mental health over it? Your irritation does nothing to resolve the matter or convince them of their wrongdoing.

- Watch out for being overly critical of your perceived shortcomings. Will you really improve by berating yourself? Instead, it is more likely making you anxious, nervous, and doubt yourself further. Practice recognizing attacks of the superego on yourself.

- Learn to have patience when trying to teach other people. Remember, nobody can change immediately, no matter how much they want to. Even if the person does not recognize the need to change, you may simply be unable to convince them. Sometimes people need time to make up their own minds, mull over your words, or see you living out what they are preaching.

- You need to be wary of your self-righteous anger. This will most often be your Achilles heel. You are easily offended and angered by what appears to be a blatant refusal to do what is right. At least, do what is right as you have defined it. Step back from the situation. Your anger simply alienates people from you, preventing them from hearing any good you might have to say. Remember, your anger isn't good for you either. It can lead to high blood pressure and stomach pains.

Your Quick Start Action Step

In order to grow as a One, schedule time within your daily life to get more in touch with your feelings. This is especially important for your unconscious impulses, which by their very definition we are unaware of. Many people will find that they are uncomfortable with their messy emotions such as anger or sexual desire.

You need to learn to better recognize, accept, and overcome your emotions. To do this, begin a journal in which you can explore them and get more acquainted with yourself. Some people might also find benefit from group therapy. Remember, nobody is going to blame you for experiencing human emotions, needs, or limitations.

Chapter 6:
Love is the Desire –
Type Two

Chapter 6: Love is the Desire – Type Two

The second type of the Enneagram is known as The Helper. This is because they are often genuinely helpful people. This type is most concerned with what they feel a connection to in life. This is often love, sharing, friendship, and family. By going out of their way for others and being generous, a Two can feel fulfilled and live a meaningful life.

When a Two is balanced, they are kind, generous, loving, considerate, and helpful. People are drawn to their warm and kind heart. Not only they can enrich a person's heart through their kindness, but they can help a person see their positive qualities and help them appreciate themselves better.

Twos often excel at being the personification of a good parent or older sibling that many people long to have had. They are always willing to reach out a lending hand with understanding and compassion. While they are willing to help, they know when to let go and allow a person the freedom they need to excel. People often feel the understanding and kindness radiating off of a Two, and are willing to open their hearts to them.

Although if a Two is unbalanced and has less of an emotional and spiritual growth, they may be more invested in seeing themselves as helpful, rather than actually being helpful. Due to their potential downfall of self-deception, pride, and becoming overly involved in controlling peoples' lives, they may end up manipulating others in order to meet their own emotional needs of appearing "helpful."

An unhealthy Two may sacrifice themselves in order to seek validation. They will follow their superego's desire to put others above themselves. They hope that by first showing others love and selflessness that they will, in turn, be worthy of love. However, this can be problematic because Twos will often end up repressing feelings of resentment and anger. Eventually, these feelings will erupt.

In order to reach balance and grow, a Two will

have to examine the darkness that lies within the depths of their heart. But this is not easy. This process goes against the nature of a Two, who wants to see themselves in a positive light as a kind and genuine person.

One of the other struggles a Two must overcome is to face their ingrained fear of being worthless. This type fears that they have no worth, and in order to rectify that, they accomplish great deeds of kindness and selflessness in order to gain love from others.

An unhealthy Two may believe that they expect nothing in turn for their kind and generous acts. Yet, they have extraordinary unrealized expectations of having their emotional needs met.

One of the most well-known type Twos was Eleanor Roosevelt. She was later known as the First Lady of the World due to her achievements in human rights. She would later on also be known as "one of the most esteemed women in the world." This is because she regularly fought for human lives, including those of the impoverished and minorities.

She regularly advocated for the civil rights of black people, Asian Americans, World War II refugees, and women in the workplace. Even after the death of her husband, Eleanor Roosevelt continued to advocate for others until the time of her death. It was her who pushed the United States to join the United Nations, and she soon became its first delegate. She even oversaw the drafting of the Universal Declaration of Human Rights.

Stevie Wonder is not just a famous singer, but he is well-known for his activism as well. While his music is amazing, this type Two has done much to help his fellow black Americans. In 1980, Wonder released the song Happy Birthday, celebrating Dr. King Jr. This song began his campaign in order to celebrate the birthday of this legendary figure across America. His song became a rallying cry and united people in the effort, leading to January 20th, 1986 becoming the first official federal holiday in commemoration of a black person.

Due to his efforts, Stevie Wonder earned the Presidential Medal of Freedom in 2014, the

Lifetime Achievement Award given by the National Civil Rights Museum. He is also known as a United Nations Messenger of Peace.

Twos in Relation to Their Center

The Two personalities are suffering from a loss of connection to their heart energy. They feel this deeply as if all of the love in the world has been taken away. In order to compensate for this loss, a Two will overexpress heart energy. Their superegos are extremely active, demanding that they be "good" or "perfect", otherwise, they will be seemingly worthless. Because of this, Twos repress their negative feelings, refusing to acknowledge them, and only pay attention to the positive ones.

In order to let others know that they are loved and cared for, Twos become warm, friendly, affirmative, and kind. Twos expect love and affirmation of their own in return for the kindness they offer. But they are unable to directly ask for what they need. Instead, they leave hints. If a Two is unhealthy and unbalanced, then they may become resentful and hostile.

Personal Growth

- Firstly, it is important to remember that you are unable to meet anyone else's needs without first meeting your own. Otherwise, you will develop anxiety, frustration, and underlying resentment. If you have not taken care of yourself and rested adequately, then you will be less able to help or respond to people in a balanced way. Just like how on an airplane, you need to first put an oxygen mask on yourself to stay conscious and help those around you, so too is it in taking care of yourself in other areas of life.

- You may want to alert people to yourself and all the good things you do but resist this temptation. Rather than nagging people about the good things you have done for them, let it be. Let them appreciate your kindness and thank you in their own way. If they aren't appreciative, you reminding them won't change that. All it will do is strain your relationship and make both you and them resentful.

- Learn to recognize and appreciate the kindness and affection of others, even if they display it differently than you do. People may express themselves differently, but that doesn't mean that their feelings are any less genuine. If you have a way you really appreciate affection, then you can kindly let them know. For instance, you could tell them that hugs mean a lot to you, or that words of affirmation are what help you feel loved. People who care about you will often listen.

- Before doing something for someone, first, ask them if they really need it. You have an amazing gift of intuitively knowing what peoples' needs and feelings are. But that doesn't mean that they need their problems fixed in the same way you're imagining. This will save you time, energy, and prevent you from trying to help in a way that isn't helpful. Remember, if they say "no, thank you," it is not a dismissal of you, your idea, or your help.

Your Quick Start Action Step

For a Two, it is important to be conscious of your motives, especially when trying to help someone. It is important to do good things and it's extremely admirable to help people out. But if you are doing it because you expect someone to appreciate your actions or do something in return, not only are your motives in the wrong place, but you are being set up for disappointment.

Twos are in danger of unconsciously creating patterns of codependency on loved ones. But this type of codependency is unhealthy and will only hurt your relationships.

Chapter 7: Being Valued - Type Three

Chapter 7: Being Valued - Type Three

The third personality type is the Achiever. The Threes are often known as 'stars' who are looked up and admired due to their achievements and gracious heart. They are often popular among their peers, they are the type of person who is voted "most likely to succeed," "homecoming king or queen," and "class president." When healthy and balanced, they display the best of society.

They know the value of personal growth and contributing to the world and society around them. They can encourage and motivate others to reach for their dreams and attain goals they previously thought impossible.

Of all of the personality types, Threes most believe in themselves, their own capability, and their talents. This leads them often being well-liked and successful. They know that it is worth the effort to become their best selves, and their effort inspires those around them. They are the role models of society and the embodiment of social values.

A Three strives to make a success out of their lives. This can vary depending on how they grew up and what success means to them. It may be having a secure career, making a large income, supporting their aging parents, having a traditional family, a grand house, a distinguished place in academics or science, owning one's own business, becoming a successful politician, acting in a Hollywood hit film, or more. However, they define success, Threes are set on attaining it.

In order to achieve this, Threes learn how to gain positive attention and praise. During adolescence, this can be displayed by the child Three recognizing which activities their parents or peers most value. They will then put all of their efforts into excelling in that area. Similarly, they learn how to develop or emphasize any impressive or attractive attributes they possess.

Threes are the type that most display the universal human need for affirmation, attention, and encouragement. The reason they desire their success isn't for personal financial gain or an increase in power. Rather, they hold a deep fear of becoming worthless and empty. They often feel that if they were to lose the accomplishment and attention that they would be of no value.

However, the problem is that by constantly chasing success and an external sense of value, a Three can become isolated from their very own being. They can lose themselves and no longer have an understanding of their true feelings, interests, or desires. This can lead to self-deception, where the unawareness of their own self can cause them to further pursue an external sense of worth. It is a vicious cycle that unless stopped, causes great emotional harm to the person.

While Threes can have deep passionate feelings, they rarely express or even acknowledge them. This is because they believe that their emotions will only get in the way of their goals. Instead, they focus on practical actions to attain their goals. Meanwhile, they lock up their feelings deep inside. A Three who has been made aware of their need to attain success struggles to understand what their true desires are. Their entire lives were crafted around attaining success in order to be of worth.

But this does not mean that a type three is unable to attain both success and a true sense of self. With time, growth, and developing a deep understanding of themselves, they can flourish. Take some of these type Threes for example:

Prince William, the Duke of Cambridge and currently second in line to the throne of England is one of the most influential type Threes. He holds a degree from the University of St. Andrews, completed forty-four weeks of training in the military as an officer cadet, and then joined the Blues and Royals regiment. He later completed pilot training, helicopter flight training, and worked full time as a pilot with RAF Search and Rescue Force. Afterward, Prince William earned a civil pilot's license and worked with the East Anglian Air Ambulance for over two years.

Prince William has spent time working at many charities and is also the patron of The Royal Marsden Hospital, Mountain Rescue England and Wales (MREW), and the Tusk Trust.

Oprah Winfrey, best known for The Oprah Winfrey Show, was the richest black American of the twentieth century, North America's first black multi-billionaire, named the "Queen of All Media," has been ranked the greatest black philanthropist in the history of America, and has even been labeled the most influential woman in the world.

After being born to a teenage single mother, Oprah grew up in poverty. Due to being molested during her childhood and early teenage years, she became pregnant at the young age of fourteen to a son who died soon after. After going to live with a man she refers to as her father, Oprah was able to begin a radio co-anchor job while still in high school, in which she would discuss local news. She was such a success that she was soon transferred to a daytime talk show. Oprah was able to take it from being a third-rate local Chicago talk show to first place. She then launched her own production company, and the rest is history.

In 2004, Oprah was ranked as the first black person to be in the top fifty most generous Americans. By 2012, she had given away an estimated four-hundred-million to educational charities. Oprah continues to give away much to charity and has even created a number of her own to help those in need.

Threes in Relation to Their Center

The Three personalities are greatly disconnected from their heart Center, which leads to the energy being both over and under-expressed. They believe that the loss of connection that they have with the heart energy is due to them being fundamentally worthless. Due to feeling empty, the ego tries to cover up their perceived worthlessness with pain, both from themselves and society. In hopes of projecting themselves as valuable, they overexpress their heart energy. They under express it by compartmentalizing their emotions, in hopes of creating a more valuable self.

Threes are very sensitive and emotional, but they won't allow these emotions to get in the way of projecting an air of value. This will cause a Three to avoid deep inner thoughts. If they are unhealthy and unbalanced, they may also avoid tight-knit close relationships, because they want to avoid having their fears of worthlessness confirmed.

Personal Growth

- Practice developing your social awareness. Many people, especially Threes, can greatly grow and mature by working on projects that aren't about their own advancement. By working cooperatively with different people, you can learn to transcend your own personal interest. It's not only a great way of helping others but also of finding your own identity and value.
- Threes may overly adapt to the

expectations of others due to their need for outward validation. But by doing this, they can easily lose touch with their own feelings. Learn to resist doing things solely to be accepted. Instead, spend time discovering what is important to you and what you find valuable.

- Real growth and development require truth. Not only do you need to be honest with yourself about your feelings and needs, but you need to be honest with others as well. This also means that you need to avoid inflating your importance in order to impress people. They will be more impressed by genuineness and authenticity rather than exaggerations.

- Threes have a bad habit of driving themselves to the point of exhaustion in pursuit of their goals. It is vital to learn to take breaks. Ambition must be tempered with periods of breaks of real recharging rest. You will find that this time allows you to connect with your inner self more deeply and reduces stress.

Your Quick Start Action Step

In order to grow as a Three, learn to develop cooperation and forgiveness in your relationships. One way you can do this is by taking the time to connect with people. This doesn't have to be anything special. You simply have to spend a few moments fully appreciating a person during the business of life. It can be a family member, co-worker, friend, or someone you bump into on the street.

By doing this, you will learn that you can gain a new sense of appreciation for those in your life. You will even become more loving, faithful, and self-confident.

Chapter 8: Being Unique to Themselves – Type Four

Chapter 8: Being Unique to Themselves – Type Four

Known as the Individualist, type Four has a strong sense of identity. But this also often leads them to feel that they are different from other humans on a fundamental level. They begin to believe that no one can truly understand or love them. More than the other personality types, they are keenly aware of their differences and failures.

However, healthy Fours are able to overcome this. They can learn to appreciate themselves, even with what they deem as failures. They have the ability to honestly evaluate their feelings, contradictions, motives, and conflict without denying the truth. Even if the truth is painful, a healthy Four will not try to hide from the truth or try to hide it from others.

Fours who are emotionally, mentally, and spiritually healthy will have the ability to be honest with others about themselves, even if the truth is something painful or shameful. This is because they are determined to understand their truth and come to terms with themselves. Their understanding of their own dark side allows them to more easily process emotionally difficult situations and experiences, ones that would overwhelm other people. This will also allow a Four to undergo suffering while remaining quietly strong.

Fours with an unhealthy view of themselves often struggle with self-esteem and a self-image. In order to cope, they will often create a fantasy of themselves in which they have attained perfection. Sadly, when they are unable to attain this sense of perfection in their lives, they become embarrassed and feel ashamed of themselves and their abilities. One of their biggest struggles is letting go of the past. Fours often hold onto their pain and negative feelings, nursing old wounds, and struggling to forgive those who caused them pain. This can become so severe that they fixate on the pain of the past and don't notice the many roses blooming all around their lives.

It is common for Fours to feel as if they are missing something important, even if they can't put a name to it. They see many wonderful qualities in others and feel that they fall short. Thankfully, with some self-evaluation and time, a Four can come to understand that this feeling is a result of poor self-image.

This leaves Fours in an awkward place because they feel self-conscious and different, but they don't want to be alone either. They deeply desire someone who they can connect with that will truly understand them. They want someone who can appreciate them, and their persona that they hide from the world, and not feel as if it is inadequate.

Sadly, if they are unable to attain this sense of connection and validation, over time, they can create an identity of themselves that is built solely around how different they imagine they are. These Fours attempt to comfort themselves, and try to make being "different" a matter of pride. They can tell themselves lies such as "nobody else is like me, they can't understand me. I'm special, I'm different." Yet, they secretly yearn for that sense of connection that leads them to create this identity of being unique.

Throughout the life of a Four, they may try adopting multiple different identities, testing out if they feel comfortable. They base these identities off of qualities, styles, and preferences that they are drawn to in others. Despite this, they feel uncomfortable with who they are beneath the surface. The reason this doesn't work is that they are trying to base their identity off of ever-shifting feelings. Humans are not static, we are like a flowing river. So, when trying to create their new identity, they will reject some feelings while accepting others as being a part of them. But they are unable to remain static, as this is not human nature, which leads them to the crisis of not knowing what identity is truly themselves.

As long as a Four believes that they are inadequate, they will not allow themselves to enjoy who they truly are. This is because if they enjoy and acknowledge their good qualities, then they will lose the identity as Someone Different, and will no longer understand who they are.

A Four can grow and evolve by seeing the truth behind their identity, that much of it is not true. They are not some strange being that is fundamentally different from everyone else. This will lead them to accept who they are and letting go of past resentment.

A notable type Four is Prince, the legendary musician, singer, songwriter, record producer, and filmmaker who won countless awards for his work. He wrote his first song when he was seven years old, and signed his first record contract a short ten years later. He was known for being flamboyant, eclectic, and extravagant. His music was incredible, not only did he have an amazing vocal range, but he was a guitar virtuoso and talented in other instruments such as a keyboard, drums, bass, percussion, and synthesizer.

But that is not all. Prince was also a humanitarian. He helped to create the organization #YesWeCode, which teaches underprivileged children code and give them an opportunity to break into the tech industry. Many people in California are familiar with

Green for All, an advocacy group for social justice and green energy. But they don't know that Prince was the one who paid for many of these people to have solar panels on their homes. Prince created the charity Love 4 One Another. He funded it with at least one of his cross-country tours and donated millions of dollars to shelters, schools, and communities in many cities. This is only the start of what Prince was able to attain during his lifetime. He left a true mark on the world and peoples' hearts.

Kat Von D. is an amazingly successful tattoo artist, reality TV star, model, musician, artist, entrepreneur, and activist. After going vegan, she soon learned that it is more than a diet. Veganism is about being conscious of how choices affect animals, the planet, and the people around you. Rather than teaching people about veganism by hitting them over the head, she shares what she knows as effectively as she can. But that is not all. Kat, a type Four, looks to make choosing kindness over cruelty accessible and an easy choice. Because of this, her well-renowned makeup brand is going vegan almost ten years after she started it. Through this change, Kat is showing people that making ethical choices is not only important but doable and even profitable.

Fours in Relation to Their Center

The Fourth personality type experiences the loss of the connection from the heart as if they have lost all authenticity and honesty. They are left without unique values or a sense of identity that lasts. This will leave a Four feeling abandoned and rejected. Out of all the personality types, a Four most knows that this is a lie brought about by the ego. They then turn to their ego in hopes of creating a sense of false authenticity.

The energy of the heart is under-expressed in Fours as they search inside themselves for something that is true to themselves. They desperately search for some part of themselves that is authentic. Since their emotions may feel true at the moment, they attempt to find stability in that place. But this is nothing that can last, as emotions are constantly changing and flowing like a river. For an unhealthy Four, they begin to identify with the negative feelings that seem more real than the positive feelings. This new identity is built around being damaged, deficient, and broken. But they also feel that this new identity is unique and authentic.

Personal Growth

- Don't listen to the whims of your feelings too much. Remember, your feelings are deceptive and are unable to actually help you. If your feelings are telling you something, it might only be something about this particular moment and nothing past that.

- You can only develop self-confidence and self-esteem from positive experiences. You may not feel ready for these experiences, but you need them in order to gain your confidence. You will always feel like you need more time, but nevertheless, you need to go ahead and put yourself in the way of good situations. You can start small but do something.

- Fours often wait to do things until they are in the "right mood." Instead, make the commitment to do productive work that will benefit you and others, even if it is only something small. You will find that by working consistently out in society will help you better develop your talents and your true self.

Your Quick Start Action Step

Fours often have imagined conversations. Try to avoid these, especially if they are not true to reality, negative, resentful, angry, or excessively romantic. These conversations have no place in reality, they are simply imaged and practice for action. Yet, people who allow themselves to have these lengthy imagined conversations rarely act on what they thought, it was not practiced.

Rather than allowing yourself to stew in imagined conversations, spend time living real meaningful conversations.

Chapter 9: Achieving Understanding – Type Five

Chapter 9: Achieving Understanding – Type Five

The fifth of these types is the Investigator. They have earned this title for being the person that most desires to understand the inner workings of the world. Type Five is always asking questions, examining subjects deeply, and searching for answers. They refuse to simply accept what they are told as is true, rather they will study it for themselves.

A Five will spend much of their time observing and contemplating anything from the way a forest moves with life to hard science. The more they observe and gain a deeper understanding of, the more confidence they will gain. After fully understanding something, a Five will enjoy imparting the knowledge on others or creating something new to put on display. If a person positively responds to it, then they will feel verified. The confirmation they receive about their competency fills a basic desire. That desire is to be told that we know what we are talking about.

This means that insight, knowledge, and understanding are all incredibly valuable to Fives. Their entire identity is created around being someone who is insightful, has helpful or interesting ideas, or some unusual knowledge to impart. For this reason, they are unlikely to find interest in subjects that have been well-established and are familiar. Instead, they will feel a pull toward fantastic, overlooked, occult, and unknown areas to question and evaluate. They feel the need to know what others don't and to experience something that is unique, it gives them individuality. But more importantly, to a Five, this can create a sense of confidence and independence.

But behind this relentless pursuit to gain a deeper understanding and answers, Fives have deep held insecurities about their ability to function within society. They will worry that they are unable to do tasks that everyone else is able to do on a daily basis. Rather than directly confronting this fear and attempting to gain more confidence, they stay within the safety of their minds. Their hope is that if they spend enough time within their own mind, they will find a solution to solve their problem and be able to reenter society.

This means that in order to have some amount of confidence and self-esteem, a Five must create an area of expertise. This enables them to feel somewhat connected and capable in society. In order to attain this expertise, they develop an intense state of focus on their chosen subject and heed little else. This doesn't mean that they are a scientist or a scholar though, they could just as easily devote themselves to music or writing fiction.

The Fives' chosen area of study does not need the validation of society, for better or worse. In fact, if society agrees too readily with their ideas, then the Five may feel that it is overly popular and conventional. For this reason, there have been many Fives throughout history who completely changed the world's understanding of their chosen field. Although, there have been many Fives who instead of developing their field greatly, become socially isolated and eccentric. It is for this reason that personal growth and balance are vital.

While the intense focus that Fives develop has many amazing applications and shouldn't be forgone completely, it can become a self-defeating problem when used as a distraction. This is because a Five's biggest problem is their insecurities, and the focus is simply to distract themselves from the true problem. No amount of mastering a particular field will help them answer the most basic of answers regarding their true problem if they continue to ignore it. While they are focused and engrossed in their search for answers and attaining perfection, their social, emotional, and practical skills will all suffer.

A Five ultimately needs to learn that they need to pursue answering their true problems that they have been running away from. By doing this, they will gain confidence and overtime, balance.

There have been many influential type Fives. One of these was Albert Einstein, a Jewish German theoretical physicist who developed the theory of relativity. This would become one of the two pillars upon which modern physics is built. He also impacted many other areas of science and is best known for his formula for mass-energy equivalence, otherwise known as E=mc2. This formula has been called "the world's most famous equation." During 1921, Einstein received the Nobel Prize in Physics for his discovery of the law of photoelectric effect, as well as his other studies in theoretical physics. By the end of his life, Einstein published over three hundred scientific papers and one-hundred and fifty non-scientific works. He is now a household name, and calling someone an Einstein is the same as calling them a genius.

Agatha Christie is a Five who became the world's best-selling novelist according to the Guinness World Records. Not only that, but her books have sold some estimated two-billion copies. This makes her books third on most sold in the world, only coming behind Shakespeare and the Bible. She published sixty-six detective novels, fourteen short story collections, and six romance novels under a pen name. She is most remembered for her characters Hercule Poirot and Miss Marple. In the year 1971, she was appointed Dame Commander of the Order of the British Empire as thanks for her contributions to literature. Despite her famous and well-respected writing career, she also served in a hospital during World War I. While there, she would treat soldiers who had recently gotten out of the trenches. Later on, during World War II, Agatha Christie worked as a pharmacy assistant. This gave her much knowledge into the world of poisons, which she would include into her books later on.

Fives in Relation to Their Center

To a Five, the loss of connection to the head Center causes feelings of vulnerability, leaving them afraid. Fives fear that they are unprepared to go through life alone, causing a feeling of panic. At a young age, they find that they have keen powers of observation. They over express their head energy and trust in their thoughts and feelings about life rather than their ability to actually engage in society. This is a result of a Five's desire to escape, hide away, and give themselves time to prepare for society. They believe they will eventually be ready. The problem with this situation is that you can never fully prepare for any situation, much less all of them. This causes an unhealthy Five to become increasingly more isolated and detached from society and real support systems.

Personal Growth

- Learn to recognize when your thinking takes you out of your immediate circumstances. While you have a wonderful gift in your mental capacity, you can use it to self-sabotage and retreat from contact with society or even yourself. Focus on staying connected to the moment.

- Fives often have a difficult time truly trusting and opening up to people. They are keenly aware of potential problems and downfalls within their relationships, which could turn into a self-fulfilling prophecy. Remember, conflict with those around you is normal in every relationship. As long as these conflicts are handled in a healthy manner, there is nothing wrong with them. Work out these problems rather than rejecting people and preventing them from becoming close to you. Isolation is not the answer. Just one or two friends who you can trust will greatly benefit your life, increase your confidence, and encourage you.

- Fives are often high-strung and have a difficult time allowing themselves to unwind and relax. Make a conscious effort to calm down in a healthy manner without the use of alcohol or drugs. You will find meditation, yoga, jogging, dancing, and biofeedback techniques can greatly help you rid yourself of nervous energy.

- There are many possibilities that a Five can see before them, but they struggle with knowing which to choose or difference in the importance of the two. Perspective is often missing when you are caught in fixation. This prevents you from making accurate assessments. When you find yourself in this situation, practice asking someone's advice who you trust. Not only will this give you a new perspective, but it will help you practice placing trust in people.

Your Quick Start Action Step

Fives need to practice becoming increasingly aware of when they are allowing themselves to become distracted by their confidence, self-esteem, or lives. This distraction could be either conscious or unconscious. Many will become consumed in reading, games, studying, and other hobbies. But these distractions are only just that, distractions from what the Five really needs to be doing. Learn to practice decisive action and you will find your confidence and skill growing.

Chapter 10: Finding Reassurance – Type Six

Chapter 10: Finding Reassurance – Type Six

The Sixth personality type is dubbed The Loyalist because they are most true to their beliefs and their friends. This is to such an extent that they are willing to undergo much pain, suffering, and stress in order to stay in a harmful situation. This does not only apply to friendships and relationships, but to systems, beliefs, and ideas as well. But this doesn't mean that a Six will simply go with the established systems, as they may be loyal to the idea that they must question all authorities or ideas. Whatever the Sixth type is loyal to, they are most likely to fight for it more tenaciously and for longer than many of the other types.

Sixes are so incredibly loyal because their basic fear is that they will be left behind and abandoned. They struggle with deep feelings of failure and a lack of confidence in themselves. This leads a Six to falsely believe that they lack the ability to take on life and its various challenges alone. Because of this, they rely on support from others, established structures, beliefs, and outside guidance in order to get by.

While a Six will often feel resistant to having someone make decisions for them, they can also rely on it as they fear to make important decisions on their own.

A Six will be deeply aware of their worry and anxiety. For this reason, they are constantly looking for something to use for security, whether it is a system or a person. If they are able to find this sense of security, then they may move forward in life with a degree of confidence. But this confidence is not in themselves, meaning that if the sense of security crumbles, so too will their confidence. They begin to feel alone and at a loss as to what to do.

To overcome the sense of fear and unsteadiness, a Six will try to build themselves a safe refuge of trust. Yet, the anxiety is ever-present. The reason for this anxiety is usually unknown. But in some cases, a person will create a name for the cause, even if it is inaccurate. They desire to know the cause of the anxiety, therefore they begin to believe that it is due to various possible explanations. Due to a Six's loyalty to ideas, they are unlikely to question this reasoning once they have established it as a trustworthy or "fact." They don't even want others to question this belief.

Due to their deep distrust in themselves, a Six might find a person who they put their trust in. This person acts as a mentor, a sounding board, or a regulator for all aspects of a Six's life. This person could be a friend, partner, or a parent. But the Six will strongly feel that they are unable to function without this person. They believe that they are unable to trust anything without this person's help.

The biggest struggle for a Six is that they attempt to create a safety net. Yet, never address the deep emotional insecurities that lead them to create the false sense of safety in the first place. This can turn them into a ball constantly ricocheting off of various surfaces of influence, while they try to find one that can "stick" for them to remain loyal to.

Sixes are a type full of contradictions. They are

both fearful and brace, distrusting and trusting, weak and strong, provokers and defenders, passive and aggressive, doubters and believers, bullies and pushovers, obstructive and cooperative, selfish and generous, and much more. This is one of the defining traits of type Six, they are full of opposites.

When a Six is able to finally address their deep anxieties and lack of confidence, they will be able to grow. They can come to accept that the world and society are always changing. Life is by definition uncertain. However, despite the uncertainty, they are capable of great strength, bravery, and serenity. By accepting this, they can gain the very sense of peace that they always sought to fix.

Princess Diana of Wales and mother to princes William and Harry took the world by storm and was an incredibly prominent type Six. While Princess Diana penned to a friend that she was struggling under the duties that came with her title, she also mentioned that she was learning to adapt. One way she learned to adapt was by involving herself in a great number of charities. In fact, she has been referred to as "one of the most influential figures on charity in the twentieth century." In fact, Princess Diana took part in overseeing over a hundred charities until the time of her divorce. Unlike most public figures, especially royalty, Princess Diana was ahead of her time in raising the public's awareness of HIV/AIDS, leprosy, various mental illnesses, and cancer. Some of the charities she worked with included the Great Ormond Street Hospital for Children, the International Campaign to Ban Landmines, The Royal Academy of Music, The British Lung Foundation, The British Deaf Association, The Royal School for the Blind, The Meningitis Trust, and much more.

Ellen DeGeneres is a Six famous for her comedy, television show, LGBTQ activism, and animal rights activism. In fact, in 1997, three years after starring in the sitcom Ellen, she came out as a lesbian while appearing on The Oprah Winfrey Show. Ellen, a self-described vegan and animal lover, created an outreach program to raise awareness for veganism and provide Meatless-Monday recipes. To the end of increasing animal care, she also served as the campaign ambassador for the Adopt-A-Turkey Project during 2010. She asked people to start a new tradition of adopting a turkey on Thanksgiving, rather than eating one. She was named a special envoy for Global AIDS Awareness by Secretary of State in 2011. Ellen even opened the show at the David Lynch Foundation's Change Begins Within gala. During her opening, Ellen gave a very real speech on transcendental meditation, how it helps those suffering from chronic stress and anxiety disorders, and how it has even greatly helped her.

Sixes in Relation to Their Center

The Sixth personality type feels the loss of their connection to the head Center as if they have lost all their protection, structure, and support. This leaves them feeling both forsaken and abandoned. Sixes will struggle with being unable to trust themselves, tasks they might have to go up against, or anything outside of themselves. They compensate for this by diligently doubting, questioning, and scanning for possible sources of danger. They are the primary type within the Head Triad. This means that Sixes are the most disconnected from the Head Center, causing both under and overexpression of head energy. They under express this energy by getting their advice and guidance from outward sources that appear more trustworthy than themselves. They overexpress by withholding as much of their trust as they are able. Meanwhile, they continuously question the guidance they gained.

The difficulty is that Sixes are rarely satisfied. This includes even the ideologies, institutions, and people that they put their trust in. For an unhealthy Six, they may even trust their own sense of mistrust and cynicism more than all else. This is perceived as a safer option because it is better than eventually being betrayed by an outward source. As their anxiety increases, they will continue to test everyone and everything, gradually eating away at their relationships and sense of security.

Personal Growth

- Sixes begin to get testy when upset or angry, which can be turned on others. This often results in an innocent person being blamed for something they have done or brought upon themselves. They need to be aware of their dark moods, negativity, and pessimism. It is important for them to remember that when they allow themselves to go to this mental place, they are their own worst enemy. This will only harm them more than any outside source could.

- It's important to remember that it is perfectly normal to feel anxious. Everyone feels this way much more than we might realize. Rather than trying to escape this anxiety, they should try to explore it and come to terms that they are experiencing it. Sixes should look for creative ways to manage this anxiety without alcohol or drugs that they were not prescribed. By being fully present and focusing on breathing, anxiety can even become energizing.

- A Six needs to learn to develop more trust. There are likely at least a few people in their lives who they can turn to and practice trusting. Even if they don't have one of these trustworthy souls, they can find one. Sixes need to let themselves be vulnerable. This means risking that they might be rejected and facing deep fears, but it is worth it.

Sixes can charm people and draw them toward themselves. Yet they are afraid of committing. Therefore, they should practice telling these people how they feel.

- Sixes should remember that others most likely think better of them than they realize. Most people are likely not out to get them. These fears tell a Six little about how other people feel about them.

Your Quick Start Action Step

Sixes are prone to overreaction when they are

anxious or feeling stressed. Practice learning to identify what triggers your overreactions. Realize that almost none of the bad things you imagine during these times come to pass, as well. Even if something bad does happen, allowing yourself to be anxious, stressed, or scared will weaken your ability to improve circumstances and change things for the better. You may not always be able to change events, but you are able to change your thoughts and how you react.

Chapter 11: Seeking Contentment – Type Seven

Chapter 11: Seeking Contentment – Type Seven

Type Seven is known as the Enthusiast for their ability to become enamored and enthusiastic about nearly everything that happens to capture their attention. They see life as an adventure and are known to be optimistic, curious, bold, and full of anticipation. A Seven will excitedly pursue what they want with a vivacious energy and determination.

Sevens enjoy activities that stimulate the mind and prefer to be engaged in a number of projects at any given time. This type is often widely read, verbal, and intelligent. But they are usually not studious or an intellectual by standard definitions. But they are often highly capable of synthesizing information and brainstorming, as their minds can move rapidly from one thought to another. This rush of thoughts and new ideas exhilarates a Seven, making them highly spontaneous.

A Seven will often have an agile mind that can work at a fast pace. This enables many of them to be quick at learning a variety of skills such as athletics or music and processing information such as math or a language. Seven will feel most alive when during the beginning of the creative process and often prefer general overviews of many subjects rather than an in-depth study on a single topic.

However beneficial these qualities may be, they can be troublesome in such a quantity. Due to the relative ease of learning, creating, and attaining skills, Sevens can reach a state in which they are bored. These activities no longer bring fulfillment, because they take little effort. They are unable to appreciate the skills in the same way as a person who has to work day in and out to master them does.

Sevens are out of sync with their inner support and guidance, which creates a chronic anxiety. Due to feeling at a loss for what choices to make or what to do, they have to find ways to cope. One of the ways they may try to do this is by constantly trying everything. Their hope is that they will one day find the true "best" thing. But somewhere inside them, they feel unable to find what they truly desire. Because of this, they may settle for anything else, because they have lost hope.

They may also try to cope by staying constantly busy. By going from one project to the next, they hope that they are able to distract their brain from the ever-lingering anxiety. This method is further propelled further because tasks that create positive feelings or ideas are often the ones they turn to. This positivity better helps to distract from the anxiety. This is also a well-used coping mechanism since Sevens enjoy being productive and are mentally stimulated by activity.

This can be seen in the daily life of Sevens. A child may not want to try out for just one sports team, but all of them. A teenager may pick up many instruments rather than mastering a single. An adult may choose to buy multiple cupcakes of various flavors rather than choosing one flavor. By doing this, a Seven can avoid missing out on the best of the available options.

Although, this relentless pursuit of trying out all of the available experiences only pushes their real objective further away. This objective will likely be unconscious to them, leaving them never fully aware of what they are actually seeking.

Worse yet, a Seven is likely to begin to make more self-destructive choices the longer they go on hopping from one experience to the next. The longer they go without satisfaction, the more panicked they become to find the satisfaction they long for. The end result is a person who is frustrated, anxious, angry, and tired. They may even ruin their finances, health, or relationships in search for this ever further away satisfaction and happiness.

But all is not bad for a Seven. When they are emotionally healthy and balanced, they can reach new heights of achievement due to their curiosity, intelligence, versatility, and quick thinking. They can also be vibrant, upbeat, and optimistic.

A Seven truly wishes to live each day to its

fullest. They can be the life of the party, as they don't take themselves too seriously and are cheerful. People are drawn to them due to their pure enthusiasm for life.

Amelia Earhart was known for her zest for life and it is that characteristic that Sevens is most well known for. This started during her early childhood when she would enjoy exploring with her sister. As she got a little older, she ended up at an Air Fair held at the Canadian National Exhibition. While standing in a clearing and watching the planes fly overhead, a World War I ace pilot dived down at Earhart and her friend. While he most likely wanted to startle them for a good laugh, Earhart felt no fear. Instead, she stood her ground transfixed by the red aircraft. She would later become the first female pilot to fly solo across the Atlantic Ocean. This accomplishment earned her the United States Distinguished Flying Cross. She was even instrumental in the formation of an organization for female pilots, the Ninety-Nines. Later on, she would write about these accomplishments and others in her own best-selling books. To this day, people are fascinated by the disappearance of Earhart when she was flying around the globe with her navigator, Fred Noonan.

Fred Astaire was an American Dancer, choreographer, actor, and singer. He was not just one of the most influential dancers of his time, but in all of modern history. He was known as a virtuoso due to his sense of rhythm, innovation, and technical control. He could equally display lighthearted joy and deep passion. His style was his own and was prized for being original, elegant, graceful, and precise. Astaire developed this style with his own personal artistry and from a mixture of tap, classical dance, black rhythms, and the Vernon and Irene Castle style. He dubbed his new style "outlaw style," which soon influenced the ballroom dance. Not only that, but his movies in which he is known for displaying his dancing set new standards which musicals would be judged against. During his career, Astaire produced thirty-one movies, starred in ten on-stage productions, and four television specials.

Sevens in Relation to Their Center

The loss of connection to the Head Center experienced by Sevens feels like they have been cut away from all that is good in life. They feel this distinctly as something is missing from their lives. They feel a sense of anxiety and pain that what they have been deprived of will never be fulfilled. At a young age, Sevens learn that they can ease this anxiety with transitional objects such as a security blanket or stuffed toy. But they become stuck in this stage and project outward their need and expectations for engulfment. This personality type under expresses their head energy, and in the process, trust in the external world to nurture them and provide security. It is important to remember that this does not mean that Sevens aren't intelligent. Head energy isn't about intelligence as most people think it, but rather the ability of their mind to welcome the wisdom that comes to them. This can be displayed in many quite intelligent Sevens.

An unhealthy Seven are constantly pushed into the outer world in order to avoid in downtime that would lead to a further sense of deprivation. As they go on their way, they continue to feel more anxious and aggressive.

Personal Growth

- Sevens need to evaluate and make sure that their choices are healthy and good for them in the long run. What they may think they want may end up being disappointing, not offering the source of happiness they hoped, or even damaging to their wellbeing.

- They need to learn that they don't need everything. Sevens are prone to buying things on impulse, so it is important to remember that willpower still be there the following day. The same is true of other sources of gratification, such as food and alcohol. Most good choices will not have only one opportunity to attain.

When possible, they should hold off and allow themselves time to consider.

- Sevens need to practice choosing quality over quantity and this includes experiences, not just when making purchases. A true quality experience can only be enjoyed when a person's full attention is on it, not when their mind is wandering from one activity to the next. By constantly looking for the next thing, a person is sabotaging themselves.

- It's important for Sevens to recognize that they are impulsive. They need to develop habits of observing these impulses, rather than willingly giving into them. This entails allowing most of the impulses to pass by and waiting until later to properly judge whether or not it is something worth acting on.

Your Quick Start Action Step

Sevens need to practice listening to people other than themselves. They will often find these people incredibly interesting and they can learn new things that might open new opportunities for them. They should practice appreciating solitude and silence as well. It is important to learn that they don't have to protect themselves from anxiety by using distraction as a tool.

By learning to live with less external stimuli, a Seven will find they can better learn to trust themselves. Their happiness will increase as they will be more satisfied.

Chapter 12:
Protecting Oneself
– Type Eight

Chapter 12: Protecting Oneself – Type Eight

The type who most enjoys taking on a challenge, and thus dubbed the Challenger, is type Eight. But not only do they enjoy challenging themselves, but they also enjoy challenging those around them. They are known to be charismatic and able to easily persuade others into these challenges. Whether that is to start a company, become a politician, or begins an activism campaign and charity, type Eight excels in convincing people to take it on.

An Eight is vivacious and has enormous willpower. It is by exercising these strengths that they will feel most alive. Paired with their boundless energy, they attempt to leave their mark on the world, their loved ones, and anything they can get their hands on. At an early age, an Eight will begin to strive to develop a fortified will, endurance, strength, and persistence to attain their goals.

One of their basic fears is someone having power or control over them. Therefore, much of their behavior can be linked back to this fear. In order to prevent someone from taking control of them, an Eight will look to gain however much power they can in life. It could manifest financially, physically, sexually, or in other ways. This doesn't mean that they will necessarily be a multimillionaire. An Eight could just as easily be a gardener, a general, manager, librarian, pastor, or author. It is not the job title, rather that they are "in charge" of their position and leaving an impact on their chosen sphere.

More than any other type in the Enneagram, Eights will stand alone. Due to their desire to remain independent, they refuse to be "indebted" to people.

They often ignore any concern, shame, or fear of the consequences of their actions. An Eight will most likely know what people think of them, but they pay it little attention and don't allow it to sway them. Instead, they will rely upon the force of will and determination in attaining their goal.

While every type may fear physical harm to certain extents, for an Eight the fear of losing their control or power is much more dominant. They are much more likely to take a physical beating without complaint than risk being harmed in other ways. They hold a deep fear that someone might hurt them emotionally. In order to prevent themselves from being hurt in this way, they often keep people at an emotional distance. They may appear tough and unbreakable, but in reality, their heart is covered in armor to protect its vulnerability.

Those few people who are close to an Eight might become increasingly unsatisfied. This is because the Eight is extremely proactive and industrious, which often leads to them losing contact with the few people they allow into their lives. The Eight is simply confused by this because they don't understand why their family would be complaining when they are working so hard to make an income. They begin to feel misunderstood and may even further distance themselves from people. An Eight simply wishes to protect their heart by brandishing it with a tough and imposing armor.

Despite this, they still have emotions. Beneath the armor that they hide so well, an Eight will often feel vulnerable, rejected, and hurt. Yet, they are unable to talk about this or even admit it to themselves, because they have such a fear of vulnerability. Eights have such a fear of rejection that they attempt to defend themselves or even reject others before they themselves can be hurt. This causes many Eights to struggle to connect with anyone or even love anyone. Because they feel that by loving someone, they are giving that person power over.

However, when an Eight is emotionally healthy and balanced, they are hard-working, resourceful, and have a strong inner drive. They aren't willing to sit around and wait for life to happen to them. Instead, they will take the initiative in both life and business and work to attain their goals with an amazing passion. They are well grounded, honorable, decisive, have an abundance of common sense, and overall natural born leaders. They can accept that they simply are unable to please everyone, and are willing to work toward a goal despite a few naysayers. Most of all, they see the importance of taking care of those who are within their care or under their charge. They wish to lead without favoritism and create a better world for all.

There have been many impactful type Eights throughout history. One of these was Dr. Martin Luther King Jr. He was an American activist, Baptist pastor, and one of the leaders and spokespersons of the civil rights movement. Dr. King Jr. inspired change all over the country and was able to do all of this through non-violent methods. All across the country, he organized civil rights activism in which he spoke on his faith, organized civil disobedience, and encouraged people to protest without violence. He is most known for the Montgomery bus boycott, the March on Washington where he gave his "I Have a Dream" speech, and the Selma march. In his final years north of Chicago, Dr. King Jr.

expanded his focus to speak on his opposition of the Vietnam War and poverty. He was then assassinated on April 4, 1964, in Memphis, Tennessee. His murder led to riots across the country. During his life, Dr. King Jr. was awarded the Nobel Peace Prize. Posthumously, he was also awarded the Congressional Gold Medal and Presidential Medal of Freedom. His birthday is now celebrated as a federal holiday, many streets have been renamed after his legacy and the Martin Luther King Jr. Memorial was dedicated to him in 2011.

Eights in Relation to Their Center

In order to expand their ego, Eights over express their belly energy. It is as if they are saying that anything falling within their field of vision is automatically theirs. If anyone attempts to claim one of the things an Eight claims as their own, then they are doing so at their own risk.

This happens because Eights feel that something terrible was done to them. They feel violated because they have lost all sense of trust in their right to belong. In order to prevent these perceived slights from happening again, the ego protects itself.

For an unhealthy Eight, they may believe it is better to fight back before a fight even starts. They believe that by staying on the offensive, they can protect themselves.

Personal Growth

- It may be out of their nature, but in order to attain a balanced and emotionally healthy state, it's important for Eights to practice yielding to others. This doesn't mean they have to become a pushover, but it's vital to learn that they don't always have to control everything. They will soon learn that often little is actually at stake in these circumstances, meaning that others can have their way within an Eight sacrificing their needs to power. It is a dangerous sign when an Eight finds that they want to dominate everyone all the time. This means that their ego is inflating, which will eventually worsen conflicts.

- It's important for Eights to remember that the world isn't against them. In fact, many people in their lives care about them. But due to an Eight's fixation on control, it makes it difficult for these people to remain close to them. Eights need to practice letting others display affection toward them and displaying it themselves. This won't make them weak, but rather will only prove that the strength and support they possess is real.

- It may seem that everyone is against them to an Eight, but it's important to fight back against this false idea. By believing that everyone is out to get them, an Eight will only further alienate themselves confirming their own fears. Instead, Eights should practice letting those who support them how important they are in their lives.

- Eights often desire to be completely self-reliant, depending on nobody or anything. Yet they don't see that they are relying on many people.
In business, an Eight will have to rely on their co-workers or employees in order to get the job done. Even if it seems that the Eights aren't depending on them, they are. After all, finding competent co-workers or employees that will put up with a domineering boss or manager isn't always easy. After alienating everyone around them, Eights are often pushed into domineering even further and become untrustworthy. When this happens, they have good reason to believe that others aren't loyal to them, because they haven't proven themselves of someone worthy of that loyalty. Whether in business or personal life, self-reliance is an illusion.

- Eights often believe that having power in the way of wealth, physical strength, or position will allow them to do whatever they want. They believe that it will make them important and lead people to follow their orders. But this sense of power is almost always overvalued.

It's important to remember that the people who are attracted to them for the power don't care about the Eight for who they really are. Likewise, an Eight is unlikely to respect or truly care about a person who was only attracted to the power.

Your Quick Start Action Step

It may be difficult and feel unnatural, but practice acting with self-restraint. True strength isn't shown by domineering others with your will, but rather by holding back even when you could. An Eight's true power isn't in their aggression, but rather in their ability to uplift and inspire others to reach their full potential. You can be at your best when you take charge to help all those around you through a crisis.

It may be hard to believe, but people are unlikely to take advantage of you when you are securing their loyalty and devotion by showing kindness. Selfless acts of leadership gain loyalty much more than throwing your weight around.

Chapter 13: Having Peace of Mind – Type Nine

Chapter 13: Having Peace of Mind – Type Nine

The Ninth and final type is the Peacemaker. As the name suggests, more than any other type, they are most likely to seek external and internal peace, both for themselves and for others. They tirelessly work in order to maintain a peaceful mind, environment, and harmony throughout their world. This desire often draws them to spirituality. Nines feel a deep tug at their heart for connection, both spiritually and with other people.

While more prone to spirituality, Nines tend to disengage and remote. They can often be out of touch with their instinctual energies. In order to compensate for this, a Nine will often retreat into their inner mind and fantasies. Because of this, they may mistakenly think of themselves as a two, Four, Five, or Seven.

Due to a Nine's energy being out of balance, they often end up causing their own psyche harm. This happens when their own instinctive energies turn against oneself, which requires the Nine to lock away their own abilities until their psyche becomes static and stagnant. They turn from a flowing and fresh river into a stagnant pond in the summer's heat.

The Nine is also sometimes referred to as the Crown of the Enneagram. This is due to it fitting like a jewel atop a crown, as it tops the Enneagram figure. Nines seem to include the whole of the nine personality types within themselves. They can display the idealism of Ones, generosity or Twos, the creativity of Fours, the strength of Eights, and more. This is ironic because the only type the Nine is unlike is themselves. This can cause fear in the Nines, making them feel that they must assert their individuality against others. Yet, they would simply prefer to enjoy a quiet life in their daydreams.

To this end, Nines can ignore the distasteful and disturbing parts of life. By numbing away the blemishes in life, they hope to find a certain amount of comfort and peace of mind. More than the other types, Nine is likely to attempt to escape stress in life or choices by trying to find a simple and painless solution or even by transcending the problem itself. Rather than experiencing any type of pain, they will try to find a place of false peacefulness. This does not mean that there is anything wrong with seeking to live a pleasant life, only in Nine's approach to it. They ignore the realities of life in an attempt to escape. They can be like an ostrich sticking its head in the sand. An emotionally healthy and balanced Nine can come to understand that it is not always possible to escape the tragedies and suffering in life by hiding in spirituality. While spirituality is important and has its place, it is not meant to deny events, hurt, or the world.

An iconic example of a Nine is none other than Audrey Hepburn. She was a famed British actress, dancer, model, and a humanitarian. Not only was she a film and fashion icon during her time, but is still recognized as such to this day. She is even listed as the third greatest female screen legend during the Golden Age of Hollywood by The American Film Institute. But her career involved more than acting, dancing, and modeling. Hepburn worked extensively for the United Nations International Children's Emergency Fund as a Goodwill Ambassador, where she traveled across the world to aid in her Humanitarian efforts. Due to her work with the UNICEF, she was later awarded the Presidential Medal of Freedom. During her early life, Hepburn even performed dance performances to help fund the Dutch resistance during World War II.

Many people have fond memories of traveling to Disney as children or at least watching Disney cartoons. This was all possible thanks to Walter Disney. He was a Nine that was shy and self-deprecating but put on a warmer and welcoming persona on film. He is the image of success in America, for his entrepreneurship, film production, animation, and voice acting roles.

Nines in Relation to Their Center

Out of all the types in the belly Center, Nines

are the most disconnected. This causes them to both over and under express their belly energy. They find their own belly energy deeply uncomfortable and untrustworthy. This is because its primal nature threatens their vital peace of mind. For this reason, Nines both repress their belly energy and push it outward in order to remain in control of their autonomy. Due to their loss of feeling grounded, Nines often feel that they are living in a dreamlike state that doesn't fully exist. This state of vague existence is used to keep anything that may upset their peace of mind at a distance. The disconnection from the belly Center makes them feel like they've lost connection with society and life itself. In order to remain powerful and energetic, the Nines expand all of their belly energy to maintain the ego's need for balance and peace.

Personal Growth

- It's important for Nines to practice exerting themselves. Rather than turning people out or daydreaming, Nines need to learn to truly focus on what is happening and being said. Rather than escaping the world, it's vital to become an active participant. By becoming more emotionally and mentally engaged, Nines can become more balanced.

- While it can be extremely painful and hard to examine honestly, Nines need to learn to honestly look to see how they have contributed to the problems within failed friendships, marriages, or relationships with their children. It isn't easy to examine these troubled relationships, especially because the people it involves are precious to a Nine. These feelings of love and caring have given them much of their self-esteem and identity. Yet, if they truly care about the other, then they must examine any role they may have played in causing the conflict. Rather than avoiding the issue, a Nine must sacrifice their temporary peace of mind in order to heal the relationship and gain a long-term peace of mind.

- Nines must recognize that they have a tendency to go with the flow in order to keep the peace and be kind. But constantly acquiescing to the will of others isn't the type of satisfying relationship that is fulfilling. It's important to realize that it's impossible to truly share a deep and loving relationship if they are unable to fully be honest with themselves and others. In order to be truly there for others, it is important for Nines to be true to themselves and open about their own needs and desires.

- Rather than hiding from negativity, Nines must come to recognize their anxiety, aggression, anger, and other seemingly negative emotions. These emotions and impulses are just as much a part of them as the positive ones are. Even if a Nine is ignoring these, they will still affect them both emotionally and physically. By having these negative emotions leak out without their realization, it will affect the harmony and peace within their relationships. Rather than burying everything, it's important to be honest and aware.

Your Quick Start Action Step

In order to become more aware of body and mind, practice exercising frequently. Many Nines believe that because they are always on the go and running errands, they don't need exercise. But this isn't true. By exercising regularly, Nines can develop not only a better awareness of their own feelings but can increase their self-discipline as well.

By developing a deeper awareness of their bodies, Nines can learn to focus their attention and concentration on other important areas of life and find ways to manage their aggression.

Chapter 14: Putting it All Together

Chapter 14: Putting it All Together

When learning about the Enneagram, some people tend to separate it into nine different types within their mind. While it is true that there are nine types, these are not completely separate. It isn't uncommon to find aspects of yourself within all nine types, especially once you become more emotionally and spiritually healthy and balanced. Although, one type will be the closest to you and that is your dominant type.

From early childhood, everyone develops a dominant personality type. It could be any of the nine types. The factors that affect this are widely agreed to be pre-natal factors and inborn temperament. We don't develop the dominant type over time. Rather, we are born with it and as we age, it becomes more obvious which we have. This inborn temperament and personality will greatly influence how we learn throughout childhood and how we adapt to difficult situations. It can even unconsciously how we bond with, react to, and feel about our parents and other figures in our childhood. This will become especially apparent when a child reaches the age of four or five years old, and their consciousness and developed enough so that their personality is evident.

There are a few more important aspects to keep in mind about the nine personality types of the Enneagram:

1. When reading over the description of your personality type, you will find that not everything applies to you at all points in time. This is because we are constantly changing and flowing depending on our emotions, how spiritually healthy we are, and any negative traits we may have picked up. You will find that when you are either extremely unhealthy or really balanced, your individual personality will alter more from the set description. This is due to the Line of Growth and Line of

Stress that we discussed earlier.

2. People often try to fit men and women into boxes. They believe that certain genders are more prone to one personality type than another. However, the Enneagram personality types are not separated by gender and are universal. One gender is not more likely to be, say a Nine, than another gender. The types are not separated by femininity or masculinity.

3. While it may seem that certain people change personality types over time, this is not possible. Instead, they may have originally been mistyped, they may be displaying more characteristics of their wing type, or they may be showing characteristics from their Line of Growth or Line of Stress.

4. The types may each have a number assigned to them, but one number is no better than another. There is no reason to feel inferior or superior if you are a Nine, a One, a Five, or any other

number. There is no significance in having a large number or a small number.

5. Likewise, there is nothing to be ashamed about when reading the weaknesses of your personality type. Remember, all of the types have both weaknesses and strengths. If you were another personality type, that would not change.

6. The reason that each personality type is assigned a number is because this is a way to differentiate them without implying one is better than another. Numbers are void of differentiating value, so it is able to help identify yourself with an unbiased label.

7. If you find your personality type doesn't fit after taking the test, look at your other high scoring profiles and see if one of them fit better. One of those may be either your dominant personality type or a highly prominent wing personality.

Each type has its own unique way of managing their emotions and coping with the ego's effect on the Center. In order to use the Enneagram to grow in your daily life, you need to understand how it affects you personally. This includes with your wings, Line of Growth, and Line of Stress. Below let's have a look at how we deal with this with solely our dominant personality type.

- Ones hope to gain control over their emotions by repressing their energy and anger. Ones feel that they absolutely must control their impulses, instincts, and anger at all times. To this end, they direct their energies with the help of their superego.

- Twos feel a strong sense of shame and they attempt to control this by gaining the approval of others. They hope that by convincing others that they are good people, they will be able to convince themselves of this as well. To this end, they repress all of their negative emotions of anger and resentment and instead focus on the positive ones that reinforce their hopes of being "good."

- Threes are often the most out of touch with their feelings of shame and inadequacy. They try to become what they see as a successful and valuable person in order to ignore this shame. This leads to them learning to be excellent performers in order to gain the acceptance they so desperately require. They feel that they must escape all feeling of failure.

- Fours focus all of their energy on projecting a version of themselves that is special and unique in all ways. They want their feelings, talents, and characteristics to all truly only belong to them and nobody else. This is all done in order to control their feelings of shame. In order to overcome feelings of inadequacy, they are also known to create a false romantic fantasy life. In this version that they falsely created, they are able to escape all that troubles or disinterests in life.

- Fives have a deep fear of society, the world at large, and their ability to cope with it. Therefore, they deal with their fears by withdrawing from the world altogether. They are known to become loners, isolated, and secretive. Instead, they use their minds to think on the world and analyze its mysteries and problems. Their hope is that by doing this they will eventually come to understand the world and be able to interact within it without mistakes. But they are never able to gain all of the knowledge required for this, so instead, they lock themselves away.

- Sixes show the most fear of the Triad within their Center, especially in the form of anxiety. Because of this, they are the most out of touch with their confidence. They struggle to trust themselves and instead look for an outside source to guide them. This may be another person, jobs, beliefs, authorities, or a number of other sources of security. Despite these sources of security, they will continue to feel anxious with a lack of trust. Sixes may also try to impulsively deal with their anxiety by confronting it directly, hoping that this will give them some measure of freedom.

- Sevens experience a deep fear regarding pain, deprivation, and loss. This results in a general anxiety that they try to avoid at all costs. Instead of dealing with their emotions and insecurities, Sevens will jump from one activity to the next in order to keep their minds occupied. They must be constantly occupied in order to ignore their fears.

- Eights feel a lot of anger and when they feel it building up, they often respond in a physical manner. This could be by raising their voice, physically, or by acting out in a forceful manner. People can clearly see what Eights are feeling angry because they allow themselves to display it plainly for all to see.

- Nines have a lot of anger and instinctual energy but they live by completely denying it. They are ignorant of the fact that they get angry at all. Because of this, they are the type most out of touch with their energies and anger, as they feel that these things threaten their peace of mind. Instead, a Nine will try to focus on an idealized version of themselves, society, and their relationships.

You can't just read about your dominant personality type, wings, and Center and expect to change, grow, or become balanced. Instead, you need to actively act on the information you have learned here to experience the profound change you can expect.

In order to let this information impact you in the way you desire, you need to act on it in your day-to-day life. You can do this by journaling your feeling and making yourself more aware of them, practicing yoga or other exercises, living in the moment, acknowledging how you feel rather than running away from it, pushing yourself to connect with and trust others, and more.

This doesn't have to be difficult. You can easily spend five or ten minutes before bed journaling your feelings. You can spend fifteen minutes in the morning practicing yoga and meditation. You can spend ten minutes engaging with other people in a meaningful way, either in-person or online.

By knowing your dominant and wing types, you can find what your hidden fears are, your weaknesses, and your strengths. Look to improve on your weaknesses, acknowledge your hidden fears, and use your strengths to push you forward.

Your Quick Start Action Step

Take up meditation. By spending as few as ten minutes a day relaxing, in your own mind, and letting your cares flow away, you can release negative energy, lower your stress and anxiety, and become better aware of your inner self. This will allow you to better connect with those around you, increasingly see and accept your true self, and help you grow toward a more balanced emotional and spiritual state.

Bonus Chapter: How to Apply Personality Types to Relationships

Bonus Chapter: How to Apply Personality Types to Relationships

The Enneagram has a wonderful way of helping people grow in their self-awareness and awareness of others. This includes romantic relationships, friendships, parent to child relationships, and even the relationships with your co-workers and boss!

With the Enneagram as a guide, you can rediscover who you truly are, how you think, feel, and why you act in certain ways. This will not only help you grow emotionally and spiritually, but it will also help you make your relationships stronger and healthier than ever before. This is partly because once you better understand yourself, you can forgive yourself. But similarly, you will find that this grants you a new sense of understanding, compassion, and forgiveness toward other people as well.

For instance, if you are a Nine with a wing of a

One, then you will find that you are a peacemaker with a strong sense of justice. Understanding these aspects and others about yourself can help you realize that you are likely to hide from negativity and deal with both stress and aggression. You can have high expectations, not only for yourself but also those around you. By understanding this about yourself, you can learn to be more open and honest, but also more forgiving and understanding.

Similarly, it's easy to just see the strengths of other people. We see them as brave, talented, hard-working, confident, easy going, and energetic. We look down on ourselves because we don't match up to this idealized version of others. But if we learn to recognize potential personality types or wings in other people, we can develop a more balanced view of them.

We may not be able to definitively figure out another person's type without them taking the test. But if we have a general idea, it can help us see that they are no better or worse than we are. Having this more balanced understanding of others will help us be more honest with them, open, trusting, forgiving, and compassionate. These are all important aspects of strong relationships, no matter what type of relationship it is.

Regarding romantic relationships, many people wonder what type they pair best with. In fact, this is one of the most common questions people ask after learning about the Enneagram personality types. Studies have shown that any of the pairings can be happy and work well together, as long as both individuals are self-aware. The opposite is also true. If both parties lack self-awareness and fall into the emotionally and spiritually unhealthy habits, then all of the potential relationship pairings will suffer.

Although, while any pairing can be compatible and one pairing is no more compatible than another, as long as both individuals are emotionally healthy, there are patterns. One study found that people of different types and genders tend to end up in relationships with each other in certain frequencies.

- Type Two women often end up with type Eight men.
- Type Eight women often end up with type Nine men.
- Type Nine men often end up with type Four women.
- Type Four men extremely rarely end up with type Nine women.
- Type Eight men often end up with type Two and type Six women.

The study also found that it is rare for two people of the same type to end up together, though of course, it does happen. Although, type Fours are twice as likely to end up together than any of the other types.

Your Quick Start Action Step

Write out a list of traits of someone close to you. This could be your child, co-worker, best friend, or significant other. But don't only write positive or negative traits of the person. Really focus and try to write down a list that is an even amount both positive and negative. This will help you better look at them clearly.

Afterward, try to decide what dominant type and wings might apply to this person. It's important to remember that your assessment might not be accurate. In fact, it's very likely that it will be inaccurate in at least one or two aspects. But the point of this exercise is for you to be able to gain a better understanding of what these people may be struggling with. You can learn to not see them in an overly idealized light. Reversely, if you are struggling in your relationship with them, then this exercise will help you see more of their positive traits.

By doing this exercise, you will not only gain a better understanding of the person, but you will learn to be more compassionate and forgiving.

Bonus Book Preview: "How to Analyze People Effectively: Learn to Read People's Intentions at Work & In Relationships through Body Language to Boost your People Skills & Achieve Success" by: Steve Chambers

Chapter 1: How to Analyze People Effectively: Getting Started

1.1

Reading people has always been an effective skill socially and has evolved over the course of time to include different aspects of the human psyche, which are now treated as relevant cues.

For example, the analysis of people previously depended on how they responded to queries but research over the past century has shown that words only account for seven percent of the way people communicate. Apparently, body language is more than fifty percent, and voice intonation represents the remaining 30 percent. This chapter focuses on what to consider when analyzing people as an introduction to the book and the background to personality analysis to ascertain the development of this science over the course of time.

1.2

An introduction to this subject would be significant to provide a context as to how the science has grown over the years. It will also be effective to demonstrate how the science affects different disciplines that have come to value personality analysis to make operations more efficient.

Even in the work environment, human resources were created to oversee the welfare of workers, but a big part of this is considering the personality type of workers that would be most suitable for that particular work environment.

1.3

The history of personality psychology can be traced to ancient Greece. Since the fourth century, philosophers have been trying to elaborate on the essence of people. It was in the year 370 BCE that Hippocrates proposed two temperaments, which were hot and cold, and these led to the known four humors that were variations of these qualities. The hot and dry combination became yellow bile. Hot and wet became blood; while cold and wet was phlegm. Cold and dry became black bile. The grouped mode of thought concerning personality was everywhere in ancient thought on the subject. Plato came up with four groupings that were intuitive, reasoning, artistic, and sensible. Aristotle was also one of the foremost to come up with hypotheses between the physical elements of the body and related behavior. It was not until the eighteenth century that Franz, Gall came up with phrenology that was a pseudoscience relating correlations between areas in the brain and particular functions.

This was some of the first work that moved away from philosophical explanations of behavior and the personality that was rooted in anatomy. At this time, behavioral linkage to mental function had not yet developed fully. Sigmund Freud and his conceptualizations of the personality were published in the text relating to the Edo and the Id. He claimed the human psyche consisted of portions, which were the ego, superego, and the id. The id was thought to control the innate behavior or the primitive instincts and desires. It represents the dark and inaccessible subconscious, which contains every inherited trait.

The ego was posited to be the bridge between

the id and reality. Its task was to find realistic ways of achieving what the id wants and find justification and rationalization for these desires. The superego became the organized component of the psyche and is the moral component of the psyche.it is the center for the conscience and regulation of what drives the id and the ego by coming up with a sense of right and wrong. Carl Jung, on the other hand, added to the classification of human personality by stating people fell into different dichotomous categories that were the introvert and extrovert groupings.

Trends related to the investigation of the personality puzzle from the angle of what the underlying motivations are for the common individual proceeded during the 40s and the 50s. Not many are unfamiliar with Abraham Maslow and his hierarchy of needs. These are from the bottom of the pyramid that is the structural requirements all the way to the desires of the individual in the society and what they would be willing to do to get these things. However, this reasoning leads to a chicken and egg situation concerning what influences the motivations of people to do something and influence behavior by influencing personality, as Maslow had believed.

However, the fact personality simultaneously influences the way that a person acts depends on the motivations themselves. Overall, there seems to be no right answer as to the direction the circle flows. The puzzle that untangles the connection between personality and behavior persists when it comes to modern psychological conversations and inspires research across different fields of study.

In the twentieth century, the increased growth of analyzing people became known as psychology and led to increased interest concerning individual personalities. Apart from significant figures like Freud and Maslow, Katherine Briggs and her daughter came up with the Myers Briggs model.

They believed knowing personality preferences would assist women who entered the workforce during the Second World War to choose places of employment that were the most comfortable and effective. The theory considers Jung's theory and asks queries that do not necessarily evaluate people according to their moral standpoint but behavioral tendency such as being extroversive or introversive.

However, the different models that have been described seem to be based according to behavior, and so they skip the part about motive. They go as deep as the requirements and the desires of the person that influences behavior though they do not attain what creates these needs and wants. Behavior according to Hartman is only the outward illustration of what is occurring within the person. The behavior-based models just identify the things that individuals do.

At the time that a child is born, for example, the first thing that people usually search for to make sure everything about them is normal is ten fingers and toes. The interesting thing is what is critical to their life experience lies in their innate personality. Personality affects all elements of the present lives particularly relationships more than physical features. It is critical for one to be acquainted with them at the least so they can align congruently with natural preferences. It provides a creative edge when it comes to emotional intelligence and success in life. Looking at someone else's driving core motive as opposed to their behavior solely provides an accurate starting point through they can be understood.

As claimed, the behavior usually does not reflect what is beneath the surface all of the time. To understand the reason why someone may be experiencing an emotion such as fear or anger, you would need to get back to their driving core motive along with their needs and wants. These are the basics as to understanding and analyzing people in general.

Chapter 3: Evaluating the Different Personality Types

3.1

Personalities are grouped according to traits which are allegedly enduring attributes which impact behavior in a number of situations. The traits of personality may be friendliness, conscientiousness, helpfulness, and honesty may be significant as they assist in elaborating on consistencies in the way that a person may behave. The most popular way for quantitative assessment of traits is done through personality tests where people provide a self-report on their attributes. The psychologists have come to investigate several hundred traits with the use of the self-report approach, and this research finds a number of personality attributes that have a say as to the behavior type of the individual.

3.2

The personality evaluation through a means of testing allows for evaluation on a quantitative level as to the true nature of the individual.

It allows a means of separation from people that may behave in a similar manner in some scenarios but do not agree in other contexts. It also allows for an analysis of motivations through the results of personality type analyses. It is then possible to gauge the driving force behind decision making for the majority of people if it is possible to group them behind several labels as the label already has a framework that is attached which details reasoning and the potential for success and failure in different fields. The other thing is personality evaluation provides for behavior prediction. Now that individuals can be grouped according to already established archetypes, it is then possible to prescribe their activities and their best positions within the workforce or in a social setting. It may also be used for security reasons. Profilers in law enforcement frequently use personality assessment methods to sift potential criminals from a lineup to assess whether someone may commit a crime or already has done so.

3.3

Objective tests

This psychological test considers the attributes of the person in a manner that is not necessarily impacted via the beliefs of the examiner. That way they can claim to be indeed independent of the bias that may arise. The objective test may mean the administration of a survey that is marked and then compared against scoring frameworks that have been standardized. The objective tests can add more validity as compared to the projective tests that will be described later on. On the other hand, they could be subject to the ability and preference of the one being examined to be truthful and open about themselves to give an accurate representation. The most common set of the objective testing framework when it comes to personality psychology would be the self-reporting measure. Self-reporting protocols tend to depend on the information provided by the ones who are participating concerning themselves of the beliefs they have via a question and answer type of setting. There are several methods for testing though each would need the interviewees to give information concerning their personalities.

These can use a multiple-choice survey set up with Likert scales that range from strong agreement to strong disagreement. The objective measures include the following:

Minnesota Multiphasic Personality Inventory

The Minnesota Multiphasic Personality Inventory happens to be one of the most widely used assessment tests for clinical and nonclinical scenarios. It was first ratified in 1943 and has 504 questions, updated to 567 in 1989;

whose answers are either true or false. It is mostly used though for diagnosing personality disorders as it was first based on a sample of Minnesota farmers and mental patients hence the name. The test takes between one and two hours to complete, and the responses are meant to create a clinical profile that has 10 scales. These are psychopathic deviance, hysteria, paranoia, psychasthenia, schizophrenia, social introversion, masculinity/ femininity, depression, hypochondriasis, and hypomania. There is also a scale that considers the risk factors for alcoholism. The test was once again revised in 2008 to use more advanced methods thus reducing the number of questions to 338. It may have originally been engineered to screen for psychological disorders, but with the revisions and advancements, it is slowly being used for other aspects of social life such as occupational compatibility and even relationships.

Myers-Briggs

Source: https://www.intellectualtakeout.org/blog/myers-briggs-test-pretty-fun

The Myers-Briggs personality indicator as earlier mentioned was created in Carl Jung's theory of personality. It has faced criticism though because of its lack of statistical validity and low amount of reliability. The MBTI measures the individuals across four bi-polar standards. These include the perceiving function, which is sensing and intuition. That would measure if a person understands and interprets new information with their senses. The attitudes function entails introversion vs. extraversion which measures whether someone tends to be action oriented or derives pleasure from being alone or introspective. Then there are the lifestyle preferences, which consider judging, or perception elements. This evaluates if the individual relates to the outside world mainly with the judging function or with the function of perception. Finally, the thinking or feeling functions measure if one tends to make a decision based according to rational thought or through empathetic feeling. Each of these functions is dichotomous, so the assumption is one is either one or the other.

Projective measures

These are sensitive to the beliefs of the examiner rather than the self-assessment of the individual.

The projective evaluations are done on Freudian theories and try to unearth the unconscious perceptions using ambiguous stimuli to reveal the inner elements of the person's personality. The benefit of this approach is it would expose particular elements of the personality that are allegedly impossible to assess through means of objective tests. For example, they can reveal the unconscious personality attributes. However, there is not a lot of validity considering there is no scientific basis for the results and they rely on the judgment of the expert analyst. For many years, the traditional projective tests have been utilized within the cross-cultural personality assessments. However, it was found that test bias actually reduced the utilization. It is hard to evaluate the lifestyles and personalities of divergent groups utilizing personality instruments according to data from a particular culture. As such, it can be significant to come up with personality assessments that also consider things such as race, level of acculturation and the language. The projective measures include the Rorschach test and thematic apperception measure.

Thematic Apperception Test

This test has 30 cards that show what most would call ambiguous figures. The test takers are then asked to form an opinion about each picture such as the background that led to the thoughts, feelings, and the story of the characters. Like the Rorschach test, the results would indicate the personality attributes and emotional functioning. As such, the TAT that comes with open-ended storytelling and standardization is not there which makes it quite unverifiable. The Rorschach test, which is more known, consists of ten inkblots that were initiated by Herman Rorschach. In the test, those who participate are shown inkblots and then are asked what each of them looks like. The test administrator can ask questions about the responses like which portion of the inkblot is linked to which response. The test then can be used to evaluate the personality attributes of the individual not to mention their emotional functioning.

One of the problems with personality evaluations is the individuals may have a tendency to endorse vague generalization. That is why horoscopes are still popular because of their lack of verification. You can derive what you want from a particular horoscope as percent of the time it will mention some aspect of your life that you are going through and even then, you will have to fill in most of the blanks. Bertram Forer provides a personality inventory to the students where he gave each of them a unique profile. He then asked them to rate how well the profile given applied to them. What they were not aware of was that they had each gotten the same profile though they were not meant to communicate on the answers of course.

The profiles though had generalized descriptions of scenarios that anyone could be going through. The students went on to claim that the profile was very successful in describing them accurately. There was yet another study in which students were issued a personality inventory, and they were issued two personality profiles. One was accurate and based on the results of the inventory they had taken, and the other was a generalized inventory that could have applied to any individual. In this scenario, more than half of the students selected the profile that was generalized as their own. The fact is both of the studies show the way personality measures can give vague analyses of the individual and yet be accepted as the gospel truth. This impact is now referred to as the Forer effect.

As such, a key issue with using personality tests especially within the work environment is the potential they initiate for illegal forms of discrimination against particular groups. A big criticism when it comes to personality tests is they can be based on narrow samples because some demographics are over-represented. They may also skew the results of the tests toward this identity. That is to say that they may normalize one identity but at the same time sideline the others. The Minnesota Multiphasic Personality Inventory test was expanded to counter the bias as the critics argued groups such as Asian Americans, Hispanics, and the undereducated were not represented as much as white male Americans.

The personality tests are a great tool for learning the individual's potential within the work environment and can detect the potential for problems early on before the situation presents itself. That being said, the personality tests have also created an atmosphere that allows for discrimination and bias based on the test results. The grouping may also be used in the wrong manner if the results are handled by inept managers.

Your Quick Start Action Step:

1. Open the Myers-Briggs online page, look for the test, and answer the questions.
2. Self-assess if the results give a reasonable illustration of your personality.
3. Have a counselor give you a Rorschach test and give you an analysis based on your answers.
4. Compare the results with the ones for the Myers-Briggs test.

To learn more about this book and how it can help improve your personal growth, visit the online

store and type in "How To Analyze People Effectively Steve Chambers" on the search box.

Conclusion

You have learned much about the Enneagram personality types. You now know about the difference between dominant types and wing types, the difference or the Line of Growth and the Line of Stress, how the Centers can affect your personality due to the head, heart, and belly energy, and much more.

This way of thinking may be completely new to you. But by embracing the Enneagram personality types and working to grow both emotionally and spiritually, you will find yourself becoming a happier and more balanced person. You don't have to live in fear, anger, or anxiety.

Don't just read this book and then set it aside. Use the lessons you have learned to make a radical effect on your life, changing it for the better.

Thank you for buying Enneagram Self-

Discovery! I hope this book was able to help you reach a new understanding of yourself. The next step is to act on your newfound knowledge and grow into the person you want to be.

Thank you again and good luck!

www.ingramcontent.com/pod-product-compliance
Lightning Source LLC
Chambersburg PA
CBHW051545020426
42333CB00016B/2104